The

DREAM TRAIN

BY
TERRY TRAMEL

The Dream Train

© 2022 Terry Tramel

ISBN 978-1-66784-361-2

eBook ISBN 978-1-66784-362-9

CONTENTS

The
AUTHOR'S APPRECIATION

❖ I am indebted to the following people for their role in helping to bring *The Dream Train* into existence:

❖ My wonderful wife Beckie, for her relentless support throughout the development of this project. I did not marry her to have someone to live with, I married her because she is someone I could not live without.

❖ My son Clayton, for sharing his resources and remarkable acumen with his old dad.

❖ My daughter Tara, for her perpetual encouragement when I wondered if this train would ever start moving on the tracks.

❖ My son-in-law Steffan, for his valuable role in helping others to know about this effort.

❖ My parents, J.L. and Lena Tramel, for instilling in me a love for the Lord, His Word, His Church, and Gospel Music at a young age.

❖ My assistant, Rebekah Wiggins, for her excellent editorial assistance on this manuscript.

❖ My favorite teacher, Cliff Sanders, who first introduced me to *Pilgrim's Progress* many years ago.

❖ All the porters that have poured the Word of God into my life through faithful ministry.

❖ All the passengers that I have worshipped with and served with, prevailing in the Faith.

❖ All the skilled workers at *Book Baby* who helped bring this publication into existence.

❖ My cover designer, Benton Rudd, for visually capturing *The Dream Train*.

❖ Most of all, my Savior who I long to see and shall one day at the end of the journey.

The AUTHOR'S EXPLANATION

I f you had to spend a long time on a deserted island and could have only one book other than the Bible, what would it be? My answer has always been either *Pilgrim's Progress* or a great church hymnal. The book you are holding in your hand seeks to combine the best elements of those two influential works in my life.

Leo Tolstoy said, "All great literature is one of two stories; a man goes on a journey, or a stranger comes to town." The greatest of all literature is unquestionably Holy Scripture. The Bible encompasses both of Tolstoy's descriptions. It tells the ultimate truth of the incredible distance the Son of God came in the Incarnation to become the divine Stranger who reveals Himself to humanity.

The Dream Train also tells the story of a journey – from unbelief to salvation at Calvary then ultimately to the Shining City. In the local church where I was raised, an older saint, Sister Lucy Wilkerson, would frequently stand and testify. Often, she would break out in a song before ending with a shout and sitting back down. Almost always she sang a song called:

"I will not be a stranger when I get to that city."[1]

What about you? Do you know anyone that you are planning on spending eternity with? *The Dream Train* seeks to show that the passengers we travel with in this life will be our neighbors in the world to come.

Everyone loves to hear the songs that were being sung when they came to put their faith in Christ. Just as husbands and wives vividly recall the songs that were prominent during their courtship and early married life, so also believers remember fondly the lyrics that brought conviction, that helped lead them to the altar, and sustained them through the most challenging times on earth.

For some readers, especially younger ones, most of the passengers on *The Dream Train* may appear to be strangers to you. I trust you will stay on board during this journey to hear what they have to say - at least until the train arrives at Calvary. If you stay with the story until you get to the cross, I think it is likely you will choose to finish the trek to the Shining City.

However, for a great number of readers, you will recognize many of the passengers on this excursion because your experience is much like mine. I only recall a handful of sermons that I heard growing up in the church, but I have retained in my memory hundreds of songs and hymns that helped shape my theology. "Psalms, hymns, and spiritual songs" are not to be sung merely to make us feel good or excited. Rather, according to the Apostle Paul, they have a unique teaching function (Colossians 3:16-17).

I hope every reader will recognize *The Dream Train* is ultimately a theology book –theology set to music. I would like to tell you more about how and why I wrote these pages, but I must do that later, for now I hear the whistle blowing, inviting you the passenger to prepare for this journey: "All Aboard."

Chapter One –

THE TRAIN

Sleep remained elusive from me for several days. Exhaustion accompanied me all the while. At last, I nestled into a bed, kept my eyes closed, and plunged into a deep slumber. Not long after, I began an incredible dream. I pictured a great train, unlike any I ever viewed in my life. This transport functioned as part of a massive system of trains, all designed by a Master Engineer. The train made dozens of stops, no, make that hundreds of stops, all along life's way. The ultimate destination that one could reach on this locomotive existed as a place of eternal splendor. Most people called it the Shining City.[2] This location occupied a realm where the wicked ceased from their troubling and the weary soul finds rest.[3] The Shining City held a reputation of being absent from grief – a place where death itself dies. The most beautiful of scenes, the loveliest of sounds, the most delicious of tastes, the most pleasant of aromas, and the most fulfilling of activities awaited those who arrived by train at this promised land.

The Shining City and the train itself came into existence through the creative powers of The Conductor and His Son.[4] (I know that the "conductor" on most trains refers to someone who collects fares and sells tickets. However, in my dream the porters took care of this task.) The Conductor on this transport functioned as the engineer, the One who guided the passengers to their intended destinations. No one ever saw Him on the entire trip; however, passengers could talk with Him from one specific car. Some did not believe He even existed, but how could the train drive itself – especially with a record of no accidents or derailments since the initial journey began?

Although no one had seen The Conductor, people did behold His Son, The Prince. Thousands of years earlier humanity appeared in jeopardy of eternal loss because of their evil ways. The most wretched of all sicknesses – the cancer of sin in the soul – plagued every person on the planet. People became sinners by choice and by nature. Without a sinless Savior, men and women faced a destiny of doom. However, The Conductor loved His creation so much He sent His Son to our world to rescue and redeem us.[5] The Son of God became *the* Son of Man so that sons and daughters of men could become sons and daughters of God. He descended so we could ascend. He faced temptation so we could overcome. He suffered so we could be healed. He became poor so we, through His poverty, might be made rich.[6] He died so we could live. (I remember thinking that the Bible declares Him to be King from eternity and at His birth, but in my dream, people knew Him as The Prince – The *Crown Prince,* whose coronation would occur at the consummation of all things in the Shining City.)

There is someone else you should know about. I never even knew His name if He had one. I just referred to Him as My Companion. He is the one who persuaded me to board the train in the first place. He accompanied me throughout my life. His voice always urged me to do right, and He felt grieved when I chose to do wrong. He always spoke well about The Conductor and The Prince.[7] As a matter of fact, I came to find out on the railway journey that His voice sounded just like theirs. I never saw Him either. Some may think He was simply an imaginary friend. However, I never would have boarded the train without His gentle leading. I needed Him near me to counter the diabolical presence of another sort.

The Tempter also traveled with us on this extraordinary journey. He constantly lurked in the corners and the shadows, always ready to pounce on me at an unsuspecting time. His voice repeatedly spoke the opposite of what My Companion said. The worst part of the devilish fiend is that he could disguise his identity. During the stops when we exited the train, he often tried to roar at me like a lion. But once back on board, he would dress up like a messenger of light.[8] He hated The Conductor, The Prince, My Companion, the porters, and the passengers. He endeavored to coerce the travelers to board other trains, which he promised would take them to paradise, but instead led to perdition.

The porters served as "unsung heroes" on the train. They selflessly waited on the passengers to help meet their needs and ease their burdens. I never even learned most of their names. Many of them were not as educated as some of the passengers and some of them even worked other jobs as well. They did far more than punch tickets and take up money. Their primary duties included explaining things from The Schedule to the people. Not only did this document feature a list of all possible stops along the journey, but The Schedule also contained 66 books The Conductor provided for the travelers' guidance. The porters knew this writing well and were always available to inform and inspire us from it.

As for the train itself, some components seemed common to what I knew, while others differed greatly in my dream. At least eight different cars made up this locomotive.. First, the Coach Car, where hundreds of people could sit for long periods of the excursion. This larger-than-real-life car featured some seats for two people facing forward, but also bigger compartments where as many as three people could sit on each side facing each other like in a stagecoach in the days of the old west. The Dining Car featured a large area with multiple tables for passengers to eat as many as three times a day. The food always tasted delicious. A large banner hung over the entire car which read:

"Come and dine the Master calleth, come and dine, you may feast at Jesus' table all the time; He who fed the multitudes, turned the water into wine, to the hungry calleth now, Come and dine."[9]

The Lounge Car became a popular place for most of the passengers. It, too, occupied a huge area with all kinds of comfortable seating available. People could play games, sing together, read The Schedule or other books, or just sit and talk. Special events often took place there. Another huge banner stretched above this long room saying:

"What a fellowship, what a joy divine, leaning on the everlasting arms; What a blessedness, what a peace is mine, Leaning on the everlasting arms."[10]

The Chapel Car usually opened only on Sunday for the Lord's Day Chapel. Porters and passengers joined together to receive instruction and inspiration for the journey. A different subject received emphasis at every gathering. The service sessions were offered at multiple times on each Sunday to accommodate more people. The room itself featured simple furnishings; yet had a sacred sense one could feel upon entrance. On the left side of the wall a scripted banner waved from above:

"The church's one foundation is Jesus Christ the Lord, she is His new creation by water and the Word; From Heaven He came and sought her to be His holy Bride, with His own blood He bought her, and for her life He died."[11]

On the right side of the wall a similar banner unfurled containing these words:

"'Tis a glorious church without spot or wrinkle, washed in the blood of the Lamb; 'tis a glorious church without spot or wrinkle, washed in the blood of the Lamb."[12]

The Communication Car served as a place where passengers could go and speak directly to The Conductor. In addition, one could listen in on the praise, prayers, and petitions of others. People could converse with The Conductor corporately or privately. Another giant sign stretched out above this car. The message fit the activity of this place:

"Take time to be holy, speak oft with Thy Lord; Abide in Him always, and feed on His Word."[13]

The train included a Baggage Car, of course, although I never saw it. Upon arrival, the porters took our minimal possessions that pertained to the necessities of life, and they put them away for us. At night we slept in the Sleeper Car. This long area consisted of many berths like the top of a bunk bed, only a little larger. This message greeted us at the door of this car:

"Blessed quietness, holy quietness, blest assurance in my soul, On the stormy sea, Jesus speaks to me, and the billows cease to roll."[14]

I wished that sign had been true for me. Alas, I slept very little the first several weeks of the journey. However, the fault certainly belonged to me alone. The train had an unusual policy. You could bring anything you wanted on board; however, anything beyond the necessities that were stored in the Baggage Car had to be kept with you in your sleeping berth. I amassed a great number of packages, boxes, and bags filled with the world's charms. I would get off the train at almost every stop, including places like Ambition, Prideville, and Success City. I always returned to the train with my arms full. Consequently, I could not sleep at night because I had no room to move around in my bed.[15] I even carried some of the items around with me to the Dining Car and the Lounge area because I deemed them too valuable to leave in my berth. The weight of all this luggage proved unbearable at times.

Lest I forget, the train also featured a caboose at the end. (I know they are mostly obsolete these days except on some freight trains.) No seating existed in the caboose; however, people could walk outside and stand on the platform for short intervals of time. One more thing about the train – it had a special name: *The Ecclesia Express.*[16]

As I mentioned before, the Shining City awaited as the ultimate destination for this train. The other major stop lay ahead at Calvary – the place where The Prince came to die on the cross. Like most people, I wanted to live in the Shining City, but I also desired to avoid going to the place of Christ's sufferings. However, Calvary received notoriety as the hub one must go to first before re-admission to the train bound for the heavenly realm. My Companion convinced me to at least go that far with the hope that I would stop at the Calvary station.

Enough of the background setting, let me explain how my trip began:

Upon entering the train, a porter took my necessary luggage to the Baggage Car while I put the rest of my things in my berth in the Sleeping Car.

I selected a seat along the aisle somewhere in the middle of the Coach Car. Another porter soon stopped by where I sat and gave me a copy of The Schedule. He began to go over specific parts of this document. He no sooner started when a man came down the aisle and interrupted him.

"Excuse me, Sir," he said to the porter. "Can you help me?"

The porter replied, "How may I assist you?"

The man held up his copy of The Schedule and answered, "Can you tell me how to get to a certain place?"

"Sure," responded the porter. "What are you trying to find?"

I will never forget his answer. He said:

"*Looking for a city.*"[17]

The porter showed him from the end of The Schedule that the city he sought happened to be the one Abraham looked for and that The Prince went to prepare. [18]The porter explained more of the features of The Schedule before he resumed his duties elsewhere. About an hour later, I moved to one of the larger compartments in the Coach Car. Shortly after this move, three men came and joined me for a portion of the ride that day. The gentlemen observed me reading from The Schedule. They each affirmed the value of that writing. The first man bore the name Philip P. Bliss. He spoke glowingly of how much he treasured The Schedule:

"Sing them over again to me, wonderful words of life, let me more of their beauty see, wonderful words of life; Words of life and beauty, teach me faith and duty,

Beautiful words, wonderful words, wonderful words of life; Beautiful words, wonderful words, wonderful words of life."[19]

I would see this phenomenon of the passengers never tiring of hearing The Schedule read play out over and over throughout this long trip. The man seated next to Mr. Bliss, a Mr. Russell Carter, emphasized that The Schedule was more than something beautiful to hear, it also provided assurances one could live by:

"Standing on the promises of Christ my King, through eternal ages let His praises ring; Glory in the highest I will shout and sing, Standing on the promises of God.

Standing on the promises that cannot fail, when the howling storms of doubt and fear assail; By the living Word of God I shall prevail, Standing on the promises of God."[20]

I did not catch the third man's name, but he also offered some wise conversation for consideration. He especially asked a poignant question about these writings:

"How firm a foundation ye saints of the Lord, is laid for your faith in His excellent Word; What more can He say than to you He hath said, to you who for refuge to Jesus have fled?"[21]

In the coming days, I would ask myself that question many times, "what more could He have said to us in The Schedule?" At this point, I remained far from being a believer, however, I never questioned the completeness of The Conductor's written revelation. I knew it did not need to be changed or rearranged. Eventually it required a commitment – to believe it or reject it. These three men made a strong case for the former.

Rather than eat in the Dining Car, I consumed a small snack in my berth in the Sleeping Car. After a short nap, I returned to the Coach Car in the early evening. The only available seat I found this time was next to a woman named Harriet Buell. She possessed a kind spirit and seemed very personable. I had heard of The Prince; almost everyone from my part of the world had. However, she became the first person I ever talked to who claimed to be related to Him. When I asked about her background she replied:

> *"My Father is rich in houses and lands, He holdeth the wealth of the world in His hands; Of rubies and diamonds, of silver and gold, His coffers are full, He has riches untold.*
>
> *My Father's own Son, the Savior of men, once wandered on earth as the poorest of them; But now He is pleading our pardon on high, that we may be His when He comes by and by.*
>
> *I once was an outcast stranger on earth, a sinner by choice and an alien by birth; But I've been adopted, my name's written down, an heir to a mansion, a robe and a crown.*
>
> *A tent or a cottage why should I care, they're building a palace for me over there; Though exiled from home, yet still may I sing, all glory to God I'm a child of the King.*
>
> *I'm a child of the King, a child of the King; With Jesus my Savior, I'm a child of the King."*[22]

She did not appear to be a person of royalty; however, her testimony bore witness that she viewed herself as such. While I found her conversation to be fascinating, I felt uncomfortable when the dialogue shifted to my background and current state. At one point, I excused myself and decided to get some fresh air. I walked through the caboose and opened the door to the outside platform. A gentleman already stood on one side, watching the brilliant sunset taking place in the sky. I had no idea of his identity, but later came to discover him as a man of great renown, Isaac Watts. It seemed as if he were waiting for someone to step outside so he could burst forth this saying as he pointed toward the sun:

> *"Jesus shall reign where'er the sun does its successive journeys run; His kingdom stretched from shore to shore, till moons shall wax and wane no more.*
>
> *Let every creature rise and bring, the highest honors to our King; Angels descend with songs again, and earth repeat the loud amen."*[23]

Once again, I did not know what to say. The awkward silence broke at last with the opening of the door and another man joining us on the deck. The two of them knew each other and Isaac Watts identified the tall, striking gentleman as Maltbie Babcock. Mr. Watts repeated to him what he had just shared with me. To that, the newcomer replied:

> *"This is my Father's world, and to my listening ears, all nature sings and round me rings, the music of the spheres. This is my Father's world, I rest me in the thought, of rocks and trees and skies and seas – His hand the wonders wrought.*
>
> *This is my Father's world, oh let me ne'er forget, that though the wrong seems oft so strong, God is the ruler yet; This is my Father's world, the battle is not done, Jesus who died shall be satisfied, and earth and Heaven be one."*[24]

Such powerful and profound words spoken on a caboose platform! I confess that my spirit often felt disturbed at the apparent triumph of evil in the world. However, this stranger just asserted that the battle is not over yet. The Conductor and His Son still rules in control. I thought,

"If that is true, I need to pledge my allegiance to this Lord."

As the two men continued in conversation, I excused myself and stepped back inside the Coach Car. This time, I sat toward the front on the left side of the car. A missionary couple named Hine occupied the seats across from me. After exchanging pleasantries, the man's wife went to sleep, but he and I engaged in conversation. He noticed I came in from the Caboose Car and he asked me how the weather felt outside. I rehearsed to him that I did not notice because of the two men and their lively discussion. He too believed like they did for he spoke as if he were talking directly to The Conductor:

> "Oh Lord, my God, when I in awesome wonder, consider all the worlds Thy hands have made; I see the stars, I hear the rolling thunder, Thy power throughout the universe displayed... Then sings my soul, my Savior, God to Thee, How great Thou art, How great Thou art; Then sings my soul, my Savior God to Thee, How great Thou art, How great Thou art.
>
> When through the woods and forest glades I wander, and hear the birds sing sweetly in the trees; When I look down from lofty mountains grandeur, and hear the brook and feel the gentle breeze...Then sings my soul, my Savior God to Thee, How great Thou art, How great Thou art; Then sings my soul, my Savior God to Thee, How great Thou art, How great Thou art."[25]

I had no trouble believing in God. A watch demands a watch maker. We were on a train; someone had to build it. To think that all this world that these men described came from some accidental cause requires far more faith than I could ever have. I left behind some friends in our town who prided themselves on being an atheist. But I heard a porter say earlier today that a person cannot even be an atheist if there is no God. He made the point that we can know the existence of The Conductor through general revelation; however, we needed the specific revelation of the Scripture in The Schedule to know what kind of God He is.

The missionary and his wife soon excused themselves to go to the Dining Car. I stayed in my seat and read for a little while until darkness fell. The only light in the Coach Car came from just above the windows. I almost went to bed; however, two travelers came by and asked if they could occupy the seats the missionaries had used. I, of course, consented and did not want to offend them by leaving upon their arrival. So, I stayed and engaged in the final conversation of my day. The men introduced themselves as Frederick Lehman, a businessman from the west coast, and Vep Ellis, a pastor-evangelist from the central part of his country. Both men concurred that the greatest attribute of The Conductor and The Prince is love. The businessman said it this way:

> *"The love of God is greater far than any tongue or pen can tell, It goes beyond the highest star, and reaches to the lowest hell;*
>
> *The guilty pair, bowed down with care, God gave His Son to win, His erring child He reconciled, and pardoned from his sin.*
>
> *Oh, love of God, how rich and pure, how measureless and strong; It shall forevermore endure – the saints' and angels' song."*[26]

I marveled at the businessman's eloquent language. He then pulled out a card and read these words that he claimed had been found penciled on the wall of a patient's room in an insane asylum after he had been carried to his grave.

> *"Could we with ink the ocean fill and were the skies of parchment made, Were every stalk on earth a quill, and every man a scribe by trade;*
>
> *To write the love of God above would drain the ocean dry; Nor could the scroll contain the whole, though stretched from sky to sky."*[27]

The evangelist then interjected his thoughts about:

> *"The love of God."*[28]

He spoke about the splendor and scope of the Lord's love that is eternal in nature. I asked Vep Ellis what that love meant to him personally.

He replied: "*I'm in a New World.*"[29]

When I asked him what he meant, he answered:

"*I Have Somebody with Me,*[30]

...who he quickly identified as The Prince.

He could tell that I was puzzled by some of what he was saying. That must have prompted him to urge me to:

"*Have Faith in God.*"[31]

I did not add much to the discussion. We visited for maybe half an hour more and then adjourned for the night. As I walked back to my berth in the Sleeping Car, I thought of all the rich theological truths I heard during my first twelve hours on the train. As I laid down on my bed and tried to find a place to stretch my legs, I determined that the love of God surely must be the greatest of all these treasures. I wondered if My Companion had somehow arranged all these different episodes just for me.

Chapter Two –
THE PRINCE

I t did not take long for me to recognize the vast difference in this train from all other locomotives I had ridden on or heard about. The great majority of passengers on board created a Christ-exalting atmosphere throughout the *Ecclesia Express*. I had been on other trains where the name of The Prince was cursed, misused, or ignored. However, in these moving cars The Prince received love and adulation. The Conqueror at Calvary became the center of almost every conversation on the train. I discovered this dynamic on the first morning of my journey. As I made my way to the Dining Car for breakfast, I saw a small crowd gathered around a small woman sitting just outside the lounge area. I learned the name of the little lady, Fanny J. Crosby, although everyone on board called her Aunt Fanny. She had lived many decades on earth after becoming blind following a failed medical procedure just a few months after her birth. Rather than becoming bitter, she possessed an exemplary spirit and inspired virtually all who came into her presence. On several occasions, she instructed others not to feel sorry for her because the first thing she anticipated seeing would be her Savior, The Prince!

As I passed by, I heard her speak for the first time in my dream:

"Tell me the story of Jesus, write on my heart every word, tell me the story most precious, sweetest that ever was heard."[33]

At first, I thought she was asking to hear about the story because she did not fully know about it. I soon found out that she likely knew it as well as anyone on the train. Before somebody could answer her, she began to tell the story of The Prince in her own words:

"Tell of the cross where they nailed Him, writhing in anguish and pain, tell of the grave where they laid Him, tell how He liveth again;

Love in that story so tender, clearer than ever I see; Stay, let me weep while you whisper, 'Love paid the ransom for me.

Tell how He's gone back to Heaven, up to the right hand of God; How He is there interceding, while on this earth we must trod.

Tell how the sweet Holy Spirit He has poured out from above; Tell how He's coming in glory, for all the saints of His love."[34]

By this time, a dozen people had gathered around her, which I later observed frequently happened. A woman answered her, a bright lady named Katherine Hankey. She responded:

"I love to tell the story of unseen things above, of Jesus and His glory, of Jesus and His love; I love to tell the story, because I know 'tis true, it satisfies my longings as nothing else would do...

I love to tell the story, 'twill be my theme in glory, to tell the old, old story, of Jesus and His love.

I love to tell the story, for those who know it best, seem hungering and thirsting to hear it like the rest;

And when in scenes of glory I sing the new, new song, 'twill be the old, old story that I have loved so long."[35]

I was struck by her statement that those who knew the story of The Prince loved to hear it over and over, as if they were hearing it for the first time. At that moment, I expressed doubt that could possibly be true, and yet I saw that very action every day of our excursion on the train.

Many pastors accompanied us on at least part of the trip, including Francis Rowley. He received great acclaim for being an advocate for animal welfare. However, his supreme love belonged to The Prince. He responded to Aunt Fanny's request for someone to tell her the story by saying to her that he would not only share it in speech, but also in song. Standing right there near the entrance of the Dining Car, he proceeded to do that very thing:

> *"I will sing the wondrous story, of the Christ who died for me; How He left His home in glory for the cross of Calvary.*
>
> *I was lost, but Jesus found me, Found the sheep that went astray; Threw His loving arms around me, drew me back into His way.*
>
> *I was bruised, but Jesus healed me, Faint was I from many a fall; Sight was gone, and fears possessed me, but He freed me from them all."*[36]

Smiles covered the faces of those who heard his spontaneous song. Aunt Fanny seemed pleased that so many of her friends stopped to discuss their favorite subject – The Prince, who they proclaimed had redeemed them. One or two others added their thoughts about the good news and then someone exclaimed,

"Here comes, Brother Chapman, no one can tell the story like he can."

I appeared to be the only one who did not know J. Wilbur Chapman, evidently, a minister of great renown. He was on his way into the Dining Car (even as I had been) for breakfast, but two or three people prevailed on him to stop and tell them the story of The Prince. He did not seem bothered by this request. He said that everything had happened on "One Day:"

> *"One day when Heaven was filled with His praises, one day when sin was as black as could be; Jesus came forth to be born of a virgin, dwelt among men, my Example is He.*

One day they led Him up Calvary's mountain, one day they nailed Him to die on the tree; Suffering anguish, despised and rejected, bearing my sins, my Redeemer is He.

One day they left Him alone in the garden, one day His Soul from suffering was free; Angels came down o'er His tomb to keep vigil, hope of the hopeless, my Savior is He.

One day the grave could conceal Him no longer, one day the stone rolled away from the door; Then He arose over death triumphant, now He's ascended forevermore.

One day the trumpet will sound with His coming, one day the skies with His glory will shine; Wonderful day my beloved is bringing, glorious Savior, this Jesus is mine.

Living He loved me, dying He saved me, Buried He carried my sins far away; Rising He justified me freely forever, one day He's coming, O glorious day."[37]

That voice from the crowd proved right. I had never heard anyone tell the story of The Prince in such a powerful way. In just a few sentences Brother Chapman had covered The Prince's pre-existence, virgin birth, sinless life, death, burial, resurrection, ascension, and promised second coming! The number surrounding Aunt Fanny had doubled in size and shouts of praise were intermingled with applause at the preacher's passionate story. I decided to head on into the Dining Car, but Preacher Chapman continued to speak. The sound of his voice caused me to turn around and hear him once more:

"Jesus, what a Friend for sinners! Jesus, lover of my soul; Friends may fail me, foes assail me, He my Savior makes me whole.

Hallelujah! What a Savior, Hallelujah! What a Friend; Saving, helping, keeping, loving; He is with me to the end.

Jesus, I do now receive Him, more than all in Him I find; He hath granted me forgiveness, I am His and He is Mine."[38]

I am so glad I paused for a moment to hear Preacher Chapman the second time. I never saw or heard from him again on the train, but these short remarks had a deep impact in my spirit. He did not just know *about* The Prince. He spoke as if he *knew* The Prince. His closing sentence,

"I am His and He is Mine,"

...suggested a personal relationship. This marked the first time I ever pondered this possibility. Our spontaneous congregation broke up at the ringing of a bell from the Dining Car. Someone escorted Aunt Fanny inside the room and the rest of us followed. I found myself at the back of the line with a kind gentleman named William Ovens. The group in the corridor disassembled before he could tell his own story about The Prince, so he asked if he could share it with me. I replied "certainly", and he began to speak. His account echoed the same personalization as the others:

"Wounded for me, wounded for me, there on the cross He was wounded for me; Gone my transgressions, and now I am free, all because Jesus was wounded for me.

Dying for me, dying for me, there on the cross, He was dying for me; Now in His death my redemption I see, all because Jesus was dying for me.

Risen for me, risen for me, up from the grave He has risen for me; Now evermore from death's sting I am free, all because Jesus has risen for me.

Living for me, living for me, up in the skies He is living for me; Daily He's pleading and praying for me, all because Jesus is living for me.

Coming for me, coming for me, one day to earth He is coming for me; Then with what joy His dear face I shall see, Oh, how I praise Him – He's coming for me!"[39]

His testimony about The Prince sounded amazingly like Preacher Chapman's words. He asked if I could share my story of The Prince with him. I shook my head hurriedly from side-to-side and mumbled something about not being ready to do that yet. Our awkward dialogue was mercifully interrupted when we reached our places. The tables were crowded, and two seats were not available together. Mr. Ovens sat at small table near the wall, and someone summoned me to join a large group in the back. There must have been ten or twelve people seated at the rectangular table and I took the last available seat. Several guests welcomed me with a smile and a greeting. I no sooner had sat down when a gentleman at the head of the table stood up and invited us all to do the same. When we were all on our feet, he announced:

> "*Stand up, stand up for Jesus! Ye soldiers of the cross; Lift high His royal banner, it must not suffer loss; From victory unto victory, His army shall He lead, till every foe is vanquished and Christ is Lord indeed.*
>
> *Stand up, stand up for Jesus! The strife will not be long; This day the noise of battle, the next the victor's song; To him that overcometh a crown of life shall be, He with the King of glory shall reign eternally.*"[40]

After a few more remarks, the gentleman (they called him George) offered a blessing for the meal we were going to eat, and we all once again sat down. After our orders were taken by the efficient food staff, a loud voice announced that we were going to be favored with a special surprise before the serving of the meal. Suddenly, several doors swung open and a parade of children of all ages began to walk among the tables. They dressed in their best matching outfits, being led by a woman named Anna Warner. They were chanting in perfect unison:

> "*Jesus loves me this I know, for the Bible tells me so; Little ones to Him belong, they are weak, but He is strong... Yes, Jesus loves me, Yes, Jesus loves me; Yes, Jesus loves me, for the Bible tells me so.*"[41]

At the end of the long line of children weaving through the dining seats was a preacher named C.H. Woolston. When the children finished reciting their verses, he led them in a similar expression:

"Jesus loves the little children, all the children of the world; Red and yellow, black and white, they are precious in His sight, Jesus loves the little children of the world."[42]

Those little ones disappeared quickly as they reached the end of their presentation. They received a hearty round of applause as they lifted the spirits of most of the diners. (I did not see many children on the journey after that. Someone said they had their own car where they received instruction and could intermingle with those of their own age.) When they left, the conversation focused for a while on the preciousness of children as several people exchanged brief histories of their own families. As the delicious assortment of foods were served at our table, the dialogue soon shifted to the theme of not only The Prince loving them, but also, their love for The Prince. An impressive looking man named Charles Gabriel was seated near the center of the table. He shared this personal sentiment:

"I stand amazed in the presence of Jesus the Nazarene, and wonder how He could love me, a sinner, condemned, unclean.

He took my sins and my sorrows, He made them His very own; He bore all the burden to Calvary, then suffered and bled alone.

O how marvelous, O how wonderful, and my song shall ever be; O how marvelous, O how wonderful, is my Savior's love for me."[43]

I had to agree. It is one thing to love children, which most people do. It is another thing to love wretched, broken people. I remembered seeing a notice about that in the part of The Schedule that included a letter to the Romans.[44] The last two words that Charles Gabriel spoke were *"for me."* That triggered in mind what Mr. Ovens had shared with me a few moments ago while we walked into the Dining Car before the meal. He claimed The Prince was wounded *for me,* dying *for me,* risen *for me,* living *for me,* and coming *for me*. I had heard about The Conductor sending His Son, The Prince, to die on the cross before I boarded the train. However, this became the first time I ever connected the dots to consider the possibility that He came *for me*. If that were true, that would make me as guilty as the soldiers that crucified Him long ago. I thought of my growing collection of bags, many of them filled with things I knew The Schedule disapproved of. How I loved my luggage – or so I thought I did. My fondness for sinful things fell far short of the kind of love these dining companions were expressing around the table. In response to Charles Gabriel, the man sitting directly across from me spoke up and added:

> *"There is a Name I love to hear, I love to sing its worth; It sounds like music in my ear, the sweetest name on earth.*
>
> *O how I love Jesus, O how I love Jesus, O how I love Jesus, because He first loved me.*
>
> *It tells me of a Savior's love, Who died to set me free; It tells me of His precious blood, the sinner's perfect plea."*[45]

One by one, his declaration inspired several around the table to express their allegiance to The Prince. A Mr. Thompson was seated on this gentleman's left. He quickly commented:

> *"Jesus is all the world to me, my life, my joy, my all; He is my strength from day to day, without Him I would fall; When I am sad, to Him I go, no other one can cheer me so,*
>
> *When I am sad, He makes me glad, He's my friend."*[46]

I had not even noticed a woman sitting two people down from me on our side of the table. Her silence matched mine during the meal. However, she too spoke up to proclaim:

> *"Jesus is the sweetest name I know, and He's just the same as His lovely name. That's the reason why I love Him so, for Jesus is the sweetest name I know."*[47]

Someone identified the young woman as Lela Long. Her words seemed few, but profound. I pondered what she said about The Prince being "the same as His name." I had already heard the name of Jesus spoken in hallowed tones more this one morning than I had in many years before boarding the *Ecclesia Express*. His followers loved His name supremely and loved *Him* even more than that.

Everyone came to a hush when a man from the far end of the table arose to speak. He wore a badge that revealed his name as Charles Weigle. I found out later that he served as an evangelist for many years. His wife had left him because she did not want to follow the lifestyle of The Prince. The standing gentleman spoke these words through his broken heart:

"No one ever cared for me like Jesus."[48]

He proceeded to testify how The Prince had helped him overcome such deep personal sorrow.

He proclaimed his current condition:

"I love to walk with Jesus."[49]

When he finished, he asked to be excused from the table and he started to leave. The remaining guests waved to him a good-bye.

I had made casual conversation with the lady on my left. Her name was Lydia Baxter. She called out to Mr. Weigle. When he turned toward her, she gave him this admonition:

"Take the name of Jesus with you, child of sorrow and of woe; It will joy and comfort give you, take it then, where'er you go.

Precious Name! O how sweet! Hope of Earth and joy of Heaven; Precious Name! O how sweet! Hope of Earth and joy of Heaven."[50]

I found out later that Lydia would often go and sit by the exit when the locomotive would pull into different stations, where she would likewise encourage those leaving the train to "take the name of Jesus" with them. A few minutes later we all disbursed from the table. It was a delicious meal, but far more memorable because of the conversation that I heard.

I continued to learn much about The Prince every day of the journey. Not only did His followers cherish His name; they also used descriptive metaphors to communicate who He is to others. For example, the first week alone I met several passengers who did that very thing. The first was a gentleman named Charles Fry. He discovered a love letter hidden in The Schedule.[51] After reading it, he said:

> *"I've found a friend in Jesus, He's everything to me, He's the fairest of ten thousand to my soul; The Lily of the Valley, in Him alone I see, all I need to cleanse and make me fully whole.*

> *In sorrow He's my comfort, in trouble He's my stay, He tells me every care on Him to roll, He's the Lily of the Valley, the Bright and Morning Star, He's the fairest of ten thousand to my soul."*[52]

Another man named Henry Gilmour employed the language of the sea in describing The Prince as "A Haven of Rest:"

> *"My soul in sad exile was out on life's sea, so burdened with sin and distressed; Till I heard a sweet voice, saying 'Make me your choice,' and I entered the Haven of Rest.*

> *I've anchored my soul in the Haven of Rest, I'll sail the wide seas no more; The tempest may sweep o'er the wild stormy deep, but in Jesus, I'm safe evermore."*[53]

A certain Mr. Jones also used an anchor to highlight another aspect of The Prince:

> *"I've anchored in Jesus, the storms of life I'll brave, I've anchored in Jesus, I fear no wind or wave; I've anchored in Jesus, for He hath power to save, I've anchored in the Rock of Ages."*[54]

Other passengers told me of traveling part of the trip with a gentleman named Augustus Toplady, who they said frequently referred to the "Rock of Ages."[55] I, too, spent a little time with a similar describer, Mr. Edward Mote. He possessed an emphatic testimony that went something like this:

> "*My hope is built on nothing less, than Jesus' blood and righteousness; I dare not trust the sweetest frame, but wholly lean on Jesus' name.*
>
> *On Christ the solid Rock I stand, all other ground is sinking sand, all other ground is sinking sand.*"[56]

It took me a little while to pick up on the language that the lovers of The Prince used. However, after a couple of weeks I understood a lot of what they were saying about Him.

One last encounter stood out to me from my first few days aboard the train. I was sitting alone reading from some periodical among my personal collections in the Coach Car. A distinguished looking young man asked if he could occupy the opposite seat facing me. I recognized him as Philip P. Bliss, one of the men I met on my first day aboard the train. I easily obliged his request. He quickly revealed himself as an ardent ally of The Prince. He had no reservations in sharing his faith with me. Shortly into our conversation he exclaimed:

> "*I will praise my dear Redeemer, His triumphant power I'll tell; How the victory He giveth, over sin and death and hell.*
>
> *Sing, O sing of my Redeemer, with His blood He purchased me; On the cross He sealed my pardon, paid the debt and made me free.*"[57]

Mr. Bliss never made me feel worthless or inferior to himself. Rather, he remained overwhelmed with the notion that The Prince loved him! I heard him say to me:

"I am so glad that our Father in Heaven tells of His love in the Book He has given; Wonderful things in the Bible I see, this is the dearest, that Jesus loves me.

If I forget Him and wander away, still He doth love me wherever I stray; Back to His dear loving arms would I flee, when I remember that Jesus loves me.

O if there's only one song I can sing, when in His beauty I see the great King; This shall my song through eternity be, O what a wonder that Jesus loves me.

I am so glad that Jesus loves me, Jesus loves me, Jesus loves me; I am so glad that Jesus loves me, Jesus loves even me."[58]

I thought of the parade of children during breakfast on my first morning aboard the train. They chanted that Jesus loved *them* and here was this grown man of distinction still enamored with that one simple fact. That is not to label Mr. Bliss as simplistic, elementary, or shallow. On the contrary, he projected great eloquence and intellectual depth in his observations. For instance, he said:

"'Man of Sorrows!' what a name, for the Son of God, who came; Ruined sinners to reclaim, Hallelujah! What a Savior!

Bearing shame and scoffing rude, in my place condemned He stood; Sealed my pardon with His blood, Hallelujah! What a Savior!

Guilty, vile, and helpless we, spotless Lamb of God was He; Full atonement can it be? Hallelujah, What a Savior!

Lifted up was He to die, 'It is finished' was His cry; Now in Heaven exalted high, Hallelujah, What a Savior!

"When He comes, our glorious King, all His ransomed home to bring; then anew His songs we'll sing, Hallelujah! What a Savior!"[59]

When he made his final point, a man in the seat behind ours stood up and came over to Mr. Bliss. He overheard my fellow traveler and approached him while wiping away tears from his eyes. He introduced himself as Marvin Dalton. I recognized him as the man who was searching through The Schedule looking for a specific city when I first boarded the train. Through several sobs he shared a conversation with Mr. Bliss. At one point I heard him say:

"*O What a Savior!*"[60]

The two men embraced as if family members and inwardly, for a moment, I wished I could have shared in that experience with them. We soon said "good-night" for the evening. Alone in my crowded berth in the Sleeping Car I attempted to lay down, surrounded by my excessive baggage. One thing I now knew. If a person did not want to hear stories about The Prince from people who seemed to know Him well, he or she will not stay very long on the *Ecclesia Express*.

Chapter Three –
WORSHIP

After that first breakfast, my most memorable meal on the train took place at a dinner event with five other people a few nights later. The expansive Dining Car featured several round tables that comfortably accommodated a half dozen people. I arrived on time and received an escort from a porter to one of the most prominent locations in the venue. I discovered all the others already seated. To my pleasant surprise, Aunt Fanny occupied one of the chairs at our table. I met her formally here for the first time. The other four gentlemen were new to me. Their names came easy for me to remember because two of them went by James (Rowe and Wells) and the other two were a Mr. Barney Warren and a Mr. Warren Cornell. After brief introductions, we ordered our meal and began to partake of some appetizers when they were served.

Aunt Fanny thought it might encourage us if we went around the table and each person would share what blessing from The Prince that they were most thankful for – at least at this season of our lives. I did not reply; however, the others gave their approval and seemingly welcomed this dialogue. Aunt Fanny said that she would go first, and she did:

"Blessed assurance, Jesus is mine! Oh what a foretaste of glory divine! Heir of salvation, purchase of God, born of His Spirit, washed in His blood.

Perfect submission, perfect delight, visions of rapture now burst on my sight; Angels descending, bring from above, echoes of mercy, whispers of love.

Perfect submission, all is at rest, I in my Savior am happy and blest; Watching and waiting, looking above, filled with His goodness, lost in His love.

This is my story, this is my song, Praising my Savior, all the day long; This is my story, this is my song, Praising my Savior all the day long."[61]

Our entire group felt deeply moved by her descriptive speech. Mr. James Rowe spoke next. I later learned he had been an immigrant who held many jobs during his lifetime. He shared this testimony with us:

"I was sinking deep in sin, far from the peaceful shore, very deeply stained within, sinking to rise no more; But the Master of the sea heard my despairing cry,

From the waters lifted me, now safe am I… Love lifted me! Love lifted me! When nothing else could help, Love lifted me!"[62]

His words resonated with the seated circle who responded with favorable comments. I remembered the theme of "love" being central at the breakfast a few days earlier. Mr. Barney Warren, himself a minister, identified his chief blessing at that time as the joy of the Lord. He happily stated:

"I have found His grace is all complete, He supplieth every need; While I sit and learn at Jesus' feet, I am free, yes, free indeed.

I have found the pleasure I once craved, it is joy and peace within; What a wondrous blessing, I am saved, from the awful gulf of sin.

I have found that hope so bright and clear, living in the realm of grace; Oh the Savior's presence is so near, I can see His smiling face.

I have found the joy no tongue can tell, how its waves of glory roll; It is like a great o'er flowing well, springing up within my soul.

Oh, it is joy unspeakable and full of glory... Oh the half has never yet been told."[63]

Everyone loved his response. Someone remarked that the earliest Apostle in The Schedule had written of this wonderful theme of "joy unspeakable."[64] Another minister at our table, Warren Cornell, then took his turn:

"Far away in the depths of my spirit tonight rolls a melody sweeter than psalm, In celestial-like strains it unceasingly falls o'er my soul like an infinite calm.

Peace, peace, wonderful peace, coming down from the Father above; Sweep over my spirit forever I pray, in fathomless billows of love.

What a treasure I have in this wonderful peace, buried deep in the heart of my soul; So secure that no power can mine it away, while the years of eternity roll.

I am resting tonight in this wonderful peace, resting sweetly in Jesus' control; For I'm kept from all danger by night and by day, and His glory is flooding my soul."[65]

I marveled at the eloquence of all my dinner companions. These last words sounded so soothing and calm. Everyone cherished the observations of all the others. As the last gentleman began to share his choice, Mr. Barney Warren interrupted him and begged his forgiveness. He said he knew that Aunt Fanny had asked each of them to share only one blessing from The Prince, however, he had another one in addition to joy that he simply must tell us. Everyone smiled or nodded so he continued:

"Hallelujah, what a thought, Jesus full salvation brought, Victory, victory; Let the powers of sin assail, Heaven's grace can never fail, Victory, victory.

I am trusting in the Lord, I am standing on His Word, Victory, victory; I have peace and joy within, since my life is free from sin, Victory, victory.

We will sing it on that shore when this fleeting life is o'er, Victory, victory; Sing it here, ye ransomed throng, start the everlasting song, Victory, victory."[66]

The group seemed strengthened by these remarks as well. Finally, Mr. James Wells took his turn, and he found a different aspect of the Christian life to highlight:

"I care not today what the morrow may bring, if shadow or sunshine or rain; The Lord I know ruleth o'er everything, and all of my worries are vain.

I know that He safely will carry me through, no matter what evils betide; Why should I then care though the tempest may blow, if Jesus walks close to my side.

Living by faith in Jesus above, trusting confiding in His great love; From all harm safe in His sheltering arm, I'm living by faith and feel no alarm."[67]

Just like at that first breakfast, The Prince received praise throughout the meal to the great delight of all the guests. I confess to being fearful of what to say when it came my turn. However, the main entrees were delivered to our table at that precise moment, and we all shifted our attention to enjoying the banquet feast set before us. Those seated at my table all seemed to know that I had not yet been to Calvary, nor had I declared my allegiance to The Prince. They did not make me feel inferior nor did they put any kind of pressure on me to speak. At the end of the meal, I thanked them all for allowing me to join them for such a special event.

Later that night, in my crowded berth in the Sleeping Car, I rehearsed much of the dinner conversation in my mind. These people obviously had something that I did not possess. Within my arm's reach I owned many things that the world valued. However, I knew deep down inside that I did not have assurance, love, joy, peace, victory, or faith – the eternal things that money cannot buy.

Several days passed by before I visited the Communication Car. The more time I spent with the followers of The Prince, the more they intrigued me. I especially became interested in how they spoke to The Conductor. No one had ever seen Him, but they all knew He tightly held the throttle of the train, guiding it down the tracks to the final destinations that He ordained. I had heard that the disciples of The Prince would ask Him for certain things and that He would grant their requests. I wanted to see how this was done. One of the porters found out about my interest and he volunteered to go with me.

The Communication Car differed from any actual train I had ever seen. The porter took me inside where we sat together up in a sound booth. There were several other booths in this car where people were conversing with The Conductor. The porter showed me how to click on a number and the microphone inside that prayer booth would be turned on. The name of the conversant would be flashed on the screen and we could listen to them speak to The Conductor. Most of these booths were small, with room for only one person. However, in the center there was a larger room where multiple people could speak to The Conductor simultaneously. When the porter clicked on that number, we could see at least a half dozen men talking to The Conductor at the same time. A pastor that the porter knew named Martin Rinkart was leading their prayer:

"Now thank we all our God, with heart and hands and voices; Who wondrous things has done, in Whom this world rejoices."[68]

The porter told me that this pastor had preached hundreds of funerals during a horrific war time in his village. Hearing this, I thought it amazing that he was so thankful to The Conductor for the wonderful things He has done. I asked the porter if I could listen in on some of the others. He told me to go ahead. (He explained to me that if any of those speaking to The Conductor did not want to be heard, they could simply turn off the microphone in their booth.) When I pressed number "one" we could hear Mr. Robert Grant, a champion for missions:

> "O worship the King all glorious above, O gratefully sing His power and His love; Our shield and defender, the Ancient of Days, pavilioned in splendor and girded with praise."[69]

I pressed number "two" and we listened in for a few minutes to Henry van Dyke:

> "Joyful, joyful, we adore Thee, God of glory, Lord of love; Hearts unfold like flowers before Thee, opening to the sun above.
>
> Melt the clouds of sin and sadness, drive the dark of doubt away; Giver of immortal gladness, fill us with the light of day."[70]

When I pressed number "three," Isaac Watts appeared on the screen. I remembered him from the caboose platform on my first day aboard the train. I welcomed the opportunity to listen to him converse directly with The Conductor:

> "I sing the mighty power of God that made the mountains rise, that spread the flowing seas abroad and built the lofty skies.
>
> I sing the wisdom that ordained the sun to rule the day, the moon shines full at His command and all the stars obey."[71]

The porter felt so blessed by hearing every prayer and I remained intrigued at the whole process. I pressed number "four" and yet another man appeared engaged in conversation with The Conductor:

"For the beauty of the earth, for the glory of the skies; For the love which from our birth, over and around us lies... Lord of all, to Thee we raise, this our hymn of grateful praise."[72]

The last button I pushed was number "five." We heard Robert Robinson for a few minutes. He too sounded passionate and eloquent as well:

"Come, Thou Fount of every blessing, tune my heart to sing Thy grace; Streams of mercy, never ceasing, call for songs of loudest praise.

Teach me some melodious sonnet, sung by flaming tongues above; Praise the mount I'm fixed upon it, mount of Thy redeeming love."[73]

When we checked back on the large booth, their corporate prayer meeting was coming to an end. A man named Thomas Ken, who the porter knew, concluded that conversation with The Conductor:

"Praise God from Whom all blessings flow, Praise Him all creatures here below; Praise Him above ye heavenly host, Praise Father, Son and Holy Ghost. Amen."[74]

I think the porter could have stayed there for several hours, but I felt like leaving. When we walked away from the Communication Car he said:

"Now *that* is how to talk to The Conductor."

I told him the whole process seemed fascinating, but I had a question. Why didn't any of those men ask The Conductor questions or tell Him what they wanted Him to do? He showed me in The Schedule where it states that we are to:

"Enter into His gates with thanksgiving and into His courts with praise."[75]

The porter told me it is alright to ask The Conductor for specific things, but never at the start of a conversation. He then pointed out The Prince's Prayer in The Schedule as a fine example of this.[76] Communication with a King always begins with worship, adoration, praise, and thanksgiving, with petitions coming later.

We saw Aunt Fanny seated in a small chair near the entrance to the Lounge Car. The porter said,

"Here, I will show you what I mean."

We spoke to her and then the porter asked her if she had talked to The Conductor already this morning. She replied:

"I think of my blessed Redeemer, I think of Him all the day long; I sing for I cannot be silent, His love is the theme of my song."[77]

"What did you say to Him?" the porter asked. She quickly answered:

"Praise Him! Praise Him! Jesus, our blessed Redeemer! Sing, O Earth, His wonderful love proclaim;

Hail Him! Hail Him! Highest archangels in glory, strength and honor give to His holy Name!

Like a shepherd, Jesus will guard His children, in His arms He carries them all day long,

Praise Him! Praise Him! Tell of His excellent greatness, Praise Him, Praise Him, ever in joyful song."[78]

"Why do you talk to Him so much and tell others about Him all the time?" the porter inquired.

"A wonderful Savior is Jesus my Lord, He taketh my burden away; He holdeth me up and I shall not be moved, He giveth me strength as my day.

With numberless blessings each moment He crowns and filled with His fullness divine; I sing in my rapture, O glory to God! For such a Redeemer as mine."[79]

He asked her one final question,

"Why do you love Him so much, Aunt Fanny?"

She once again had a ready reply:

"To God be the glory, great things He hath done, So loved He the world that He gave us His Son; Who yielded His life an atonement for sin, and opened the life gate that all may go in.

Great things He hath taught us, great things He hath done, and great our rejoicing thru Jesus the Son; But purer and higher and greater will be, our wonder, our transport, when Jesus we see."[80]

We thanked Aunt Fanny and wished her the best for the rest of her day. I realized the porter and this little lady had just shared a valuable lesson with me. I thanked him for all the time he spent with me and returned to my berth in the Sleeping Car.

Less than a week later I heard the news that Charles Wesley had boarded our train. Almost everyone had heard of him and his brother, John. Their fame had spread across many lands. John was known for talking about The Prince to the people, while Charles achieved acclaim for talking to The Prince on behalf of people. He always had many others around him on the train so I knew I would likely never get to meet him. However, one morning I heard Charles Wesley speak to The Conductor in the Communication Car. The porter who initially helped me found me early that day and said he was holding me a place. I quickly got ready and followed him back to that special car. When we arrived, Mr. Wesley had already begun to converse with the mighty Engineer, The Conductor of the *Ecclesia Express*. We arrived in time to hear him cry:

"Jesus, lover of my soul, let me to Thy bosom fly; While the nearer waters roll, while the tempest still is high.

Hide me, O my Savior, hide, till the storm of life is past; Safe into the haven guide, Oh, receive my soul at last."[81]

Like the waves rolling in one after another, the words flowed from Wesley's heart and lips to the ear of The Conductor.

"Love divine, all loves excelling, Joy of Heaven to earth come down, Fix in us thy humble dwelling, all thy faithful mercies crown.

Jesus, Thou art all compassion, pure unbounded love Thou art; Visit us with Thy salvation, enter every trembling heart.

Finish, then, Thy new creation, pure and spotless let us be, Let us see Thy great salvation, perfectly restored in Thee;

Changed from glory into glory, till in Heaven we take our place, Till we cast our crowns before Thee, lost in wonder, love, and praise."[82]

My heart felt especially stirred when I heard him weave some of his own personal testimony into this conversation:

"Long my imprisoned spirit lay, fast bound in sin and nature's night, Thine eye diffused a quickening ray, I woke, the dungeon flamed with light.

My chains fell off, my heart was free, I rose, went forth, and followed Thee... Amazing love! How can it be? That Thou, my God, should'st die for me."[83]

I only stayed a few minutes more, but it was long enough to hear Charles Wesley reach a crescendo of worship:

"Oh, for a thousand tongues to sing, my great Redeemer's praise; The glories of my God and King, the triumphs of His grace.

He breaks the power of canceled sin, He sets the prisoner free; His blood can make the foulest clean, His blood availed for me."[84]

Hearing Charles Wesley communicate with The Conductor produced a genuine thrill. However, the greater impact to me came from hearing four different men converse with the Lord, not on the train at all, but during one of the many stops. (I knew they were passengers on the

Ecclesia Express because they wore special name tags which allowed them to reboard the locomotive.) At one of the stops, the train station sits beside a beautiful lake. After spending some hours in this quaint village, I decided to return to the rail cars via a path along the water. Less than 500 yards from the train I spied a man looking out over the lake. Not a single soul stood near him, yet he spoke with a loud voice:

> "Holy, Holy, Holy, Lord God Almighty, early in the morning our song shall rise to Thee; Holy, Holy, Holy, merciful and mighty, God in three persons, blessed Trinity.
>
> Holy, Holy, Holy, all the saints adore Thee, casting down their golden crowns around the glassy sea; Cherubim and seraphim, falling down before Thee, Who was and is and evermore shall be."[85]

I found out later his name: Reginald Huber. I marveled that a man would talk to his God even when nobody else knew he did it. The same thing happened at another time and place by a gentleman named Thomas Chisholm. I shopped in the marketplace one afternoon in a different city. On an adjacent aisle I heard a distinct voice proclaim:

> "Great is Thy faithfulness, O God my Father, there is no shadow of turning with Thee; Thou changest not, Thy compassions, they fail not, as Thou hast been Thou forever will be.
>
> Great is Thy faithfulness! Great is Thy faithfulness! Morning by morning new mercies I see; All I have needed Thy hand hath provided, Great is Thy faithfulness, Lord unto me.
>
> Pardon for sin and a peace that endureth, Thine own dear presence to cheer and to guide; Strength for today and bright hope for tomorrow, Blessings all mine, with ten thousand beside."[86]

When I turned the corner to look down that direction, again no one was present except for this Thomas Chisholm. These men were not putting on a performance for anyone. Clearly, they were communicating with an

Audience of One. I observed a third man, Matthew Bridges, do the same thing. At a city park with many monuments erected of famous people, I watched him sit on a bench and speak to The Conductor as if he were in the main booth of the Communication Car. He lifted his voice to declare:

"Crown Him with many crowns, the Lamb upon His throne, Hark, how the heavenly anthem drowns all music but its own; Awake my soul and sing, of Him who died for thee, And hail Him as thy matchless King, through all eternity."[87]

That made three men who worshipped in Spirit and in Truth off the train, as well as on it. One final man inspired me, howbeit in a different way. At one stop where I purchased more bags with trinkets that I did not need, I beheld a sight that remained fixed in my mind. One of the passengers of the *Ecclesia Express* openly praised his Savior as:

"My Wonderful Lord!"[88]

Suddenly he felt surrounded by a half dozen mockers from that city. They ridiculed his faith and made fun of The Prince. They laughed at his Schedule and belittled the train. Yet that did not quiet Haldor Lillenas. In the midst of their persecution, he stood tall and boldly replied:

"Patiently, tenderly pleading, Jesus is standing today, At your heart's door He knocks as before, O turn him no longer away."[89]

I learned that day that some people are the same in private as they are in public. This is how I knew that the passengers possessed something real. These four men lived the same off the train as they did while riding on it. The train bore no resemblance to a theatre where actors could pretend to be religious. Those who praised The Prince had been genuinely transformed.

Chapter Four –

GRACE

Christmas time became a wonderful season to be riding on the *Ecclesia Express*. The overwhelming majority of passengers on board manifested happiness. Their joy magnified as they contemplated The Conductor sending His Son, The Prince, to rescue and redeem them unto Himself. One night a magnificent Christmas party took place in the Lounge Car, which featured everyone receiving special gifts from the train and from each other. The presents were all extraordinary in vision, while not being excessive in value. The children joined the adults for this festive time of food, fellowship, and faith. Even though I had not yet placed my trust in The Prince, I recognized that the best part of the evening came during the presentations at the end. A gentleman named Benjamin Hanby opened the program with a question:

> "*Who is He in yonder stall at whose feet the shepherds fall? Who is He in deep distress, fasting in the wilderness?*
>
> *Who is He the people bless for His words of gentleness? Who is He to whom they bring all the sick and sorrowing?*

Who is He that stands and weeps at the grave where Lazarus sleeps? Who is He the gathering throng greet with loud triumphant song?

Lo! at midnight, who is He, prays in dark Gethsemane; Who is He on yonder tree, dies in grief and agony?

Who is He that from the grave comes to heal and help and save? Who is He that from His throne rules through all the world alone?

'Tis the Lord, O wondrous story! 'Tis the Lord, the King of glory; At His feet we humbly fall, Crown Him, crown Him, Lord of all."[90]

The expressions on the faces of the passengers beamed with great delight. The story they loved so much seemed enhanced even more at this Christmas season.

Mr. Isaac Watts followed the opening speaker. He always commanded the attention and respect of any audience. He arose from his chair and thundered with a loud voice:

"Joy to the world, the Lord is come, let earth receive its King, Let every heart prepare Him room and Heaven and nature sing.

Joy to the earth the Savior reigns, let all their songs employ; While fields and floods, rocks, hills, and plains, repeat the sounding joy.

No more let sins and sorrows grow, nor thorns infest the ground; He comes to make His blessings flow, far as the curse is found.

He rules the world with truth and grace, and makes the nations prove; the glories of His righteousness and wonders of His love."[91]

(One of the porters leaned over to me and said that Mr. Watts' description not only celebrates the first coming of The Prince, but also looks forward to His second advent.)

These glowing words set the stage for Charles Wesley to come and engage the people. I had no idea he was still on the train. I presumed he already changed to a connecting train at one of the stops. I heard him speak directly to The Conductor a few days ago, but now he was addressing The Prince in the presence of all of us:

"Come, Thou long-expected Jesus, born to set Thy people free; From our fears and sins release us, let us find our rest in Thee.

Israel's strength and consolation, hope of all the earth Thou art; Dear Desire of every nation, joy of every longing heart.

Born Thy people to deliver, born a child and yet a King; Born to reign in us forever, now, Thy gracious kingdom bring.

By Thine own eternal Spirit, rule in all our hearts alone; By Thine all-sufficient merit, raise us to Thy glorious throne."[92]

The above sentences were only a part of his presentation. When he turned to go sit down, someone cried out,

"Charles, tell us about when the angels sang."

This request met with ripples of approval from the audience, so Mr. Wesley turned around and shared his matchless speech with us. I was amazed that most of the crowd knew some of it, word for word, and said it along with him in unison:

"Hark! the herald angels sing, 'Glory to the newborn King, peace on earth and mercy mild, God and sinners reconciled; Joyful all ye nations rise, join the triumph of the skies, with angelic hosts proclaim, Christ is born in Bethlehem, Hark the herald angels sing, 'Glory to the newborn King.'

Christ by highest Heaven adored, Christ, the everlasting Lord, late in time, behold Him come, offspring of the Virgin's womb; Veiled in flesh the Godhead see, hail the Incarnate Deity, Pleased with us in flesh to dwell, Jesus, our Immanuel, Hark the herald angels sing, 'Glory to the newborn King.'

Hail the Heaven-born Prince of Peace, Hail the Son of Righteousness, Light and life to all He brings, risen with healing in His wings; Mild He

lays His glory by, born that we may no more die, Born to raise us from the earth, born to give us second birth, Hark the herald angels sing, 'Glory to the newborn King.'[93]

That remarkable speech would have been a fitting ending to the program, but one final speaker remained. Rumors circulated about a famous gentleman possibly aboard the train who might address us at the end of the night. The gathered host certainly felt surprised when Henry Wadsworth Longfellow was introduced in our midst. The audience greeted him with hearty applause as he explained his prepared remarks were composed after a very difficult season of his life, which included the death of his wife and the serious injury of his son during the war. Here is what he said:

"I heard the bells on Christmas Day their old familiar carols play, and wild and sweet the words repeat of peace on earth, good-will to men.

And in despair I bowed my head, 'There is no peace on earth' I said; For hate is strong and mocks the song, of peace on earth good-will to men.

Then pealed the bells more loud and deep: 'God is not dead, nor doth He sleep;' the wrong shall fail, the right prevail, with peace on earth, good-will to men."[94]

I dreaded the possibility of a lonely Christmas on a train, but instead, it proved to be one of the most memorable holy days I ever observed.

The porters posted every week what the theme of the Lord's Day Chapel service would be. I had no interest in attending some of the sessions that featured more sensationalized subjects like: (1) Is there life on other planets? (2) Where did Cain get his wife? (3) What happened to the dinosaurs? Nor was I drawn to the chapels that advertised a controversial "in-house debate" like: (1) millennial issues, (2) women porters, or (3) speaking in tongues. Archeology findings did not allure me to attend. Although I had not yet embraced Him as Savior and Lord, I was much more interested in the Rock of Ages than the ages of rocks.

On the first day of the new year, someone changed the sign to announce the subject for the next Lord's Day Chapel. One word said it all: "GRACE." When I saw that word posted, I knew I needed to attend that session. For one thing, I always loved the sound of that word – "grace." It glides gently across one's tongue when it is spoken. It sounded like the name of an elegant lady or an innocent baby. Surely it remained one of the most beautiful words in my language. A porter once told me the Greek word for "grace" is "*charis*" – which itself is a pleasant-sounding word. Another porter defined the word as "unmerited favor" – something bestowed upon a person that was not deserved. I did not view myself as being too bad to receive salvation by grace, rather, I perceived myself as being "too good" to need saving grace.

I somewhat knew what to expect in the chapel service. I had Aunt Fanny to thank for that. I heard her many times utter this hopeful expression:

"And I shall see Him face to face and tell the story 'Saved by Grace.'"[95]

A man of modest means named Philip Doddridge spoke first. He confirmed my sentiments concerning the utterance of "grace":

"Grace! 'Tis a charming sound, harmonious to my ear; Heaven with the echo shall resound, and all the earth shall hear.

Grace first contrived the way, to save rebellious man; And all the steps that grace display, which drew the wondrous plan. "[96]

The porter in charge at the chapel did indeed reference salvation by grace from The Schedule, but he began by talking about "prevenient grace." This term evidently refers to all The Conductor's favor and lovingkindness toward people even before they come to know Him as Savior and Lord. He then highlighted several examples from The Schedule of God's grace transforming various lives. He especially drew our attention to The Prince dispensing such grace when He walked on the earth to a woman with seven devils, to another with five husbands, to a wild man who ran around naked, and a dying robber on a tree.[97] The porter then called on Haldor Lillenas to share what grace meant to him. This passionate fellow was the man I heard proclaiming his Wonderful Lord on the streets during a train stop. This morning he stood up and began to answer the question posed to him:

> "*Wonderful grace of Jesus, greater than all my sin, how shall my tongue describe it, where shall its praise begin?*
>
> *Taking away my burden, setting my spirit free; for the wonderful grace of Jesus reaches me.*
>
> *Wonderful the matchless grace of Jesus, deeper than the mighty rolling sea, Higher than the mountain, sparkling like a fountain, all sufficient grace for even me...*
>
> *Broader than the scope of my transgressions, greater far than all my sin and shame, Oh magnify the precious name of Jesus, praise His Name!*
>
> *Wonderful grace of Jesus, reaching to all the lost, by it I have been pardoned, saved to the uttermost;*
>
> *Chains have been torn asunder, giving me liberty, For the wonderful grace of Jesus reaches me!*"[98]

The fact that grace reached him made the speaker marvel the most! I began to think of many other followers of Jesus who I had heard share a similar testimony. God's grace could rescue the most wretched of sinners, yet what need of it did someone like me have, who prided myself on being "good" on my own? It seemed that the porter knew exactly what I had been thinking because he then pointed out the story in The Schedule about a Pharisee and a Publican. They both knelt to pray in a temple. The former said:

"I thank God I'm not like other men."

The latter cried out:

"God be merciful to me a sinner."

The Prince said only the second man went home justified.[99] The porter called that story "A Good Man Lost and a Bad Man Saved."

The porter than commented on Mr. Lillenas' words about receiving liberty instead of being bound by chains. He said that, under the Law, the best of men remained condemned, but now, under grace, even the worst of men can be saved. He pointed out from The Schedule that under the Law, sheep died for the shepherds, but under grace, the Shepherd has come to die for the sheep! He told the listeners that GRACE forms an easy to remember acronym: "God's Riches at Christ's Expense." I thought to myself, if this is true, surely it is the greatest of all possible news one could hear.

Soon, there was a buzz that went through the assembled congregation as Mr. John Newton stepped forward to address our group. Word had spread about his past and about him now being on this train. It was common knowledge he once lived as a slave trader, a ruthless man trafficking in human lives until he experienced an extraordinary encounter. He described it in his own words:

> "*Amazing grace, how sweet the sound, that saved a wretch like me; I once was lost, but now I'm found, 'twas blind, but now I see.*"[100]

There is no other word for grace except "amazing" – if indeed it is true. And how could someone question not just one, but tens of thousands of testimonies just like his? Mr. Newton continued:

> "*'Twas grace that taught my heart to fear and grace my fears relieved; How precious did that grace appear, the hour I first believed.*"[101]

That last sentence sank deep into my soul – the precious appearing of grace! The converted slave dealer suggested that it happens when the lost human truly believes on the Lord. Grace exists as His part, a divine and exclusive act. Faith is our part, the human response to The Conductor's lovingkindness toward us. The two are interwoven together. Those who persist in unbelief disqualify themselves from becoming a recipient of God's grace. And those who receive His grace do so only through genuine faith. The plan of salvation, thanks to the porters and passengers on this train, became clearer to me. I felt surprised that Mr. Newton's remarks were so brief. However, others waited to speak at the chapel, including Mrs. Julia Johnston. After a porter read from The Schedule about grace abounding even more than sin, she came forth and addressed the hearers:[102]

> *"Marvelous grace of our loving Lord, Grace that exceeds our sin and our guilt; Yonder on Calvary's mount outpoured, there where the blood of the Lamb was spilled.*
>
> *Sin and despair, like the sea waves cold, threaten the soul with infinite loss; Grace that is greater, yes, grace untold, points to the refuge, the mighty cross.*
>
> *Dark is the stain that we cannot hide, what can we do to wash it away? Look! There is flowing a crimson tide, brighter than snow you may be today.*
>
> *Grace, grace, God's grace, Grace that will pardon and cleanse within; Grace, grace, God's grace, Grace that is greater than all our sin."*[103]

She tied the Lord's grace in an inseparable knot with The Prince's death on the cross. Grace *is* a beautiful word and concept, but its greatest expression in human history involved the spilled blood of the Lamb, the mighty cross, and a flowing crimson tide. Her constant references to "sin and our guilt," "sin and despair," and a "dark stain we cannot hide" reminded me of all my baggage – so many parcels I could not even rest well at night. I had some things hidden in those packages that I did not want anyone to see or even know about. Those possessions had become the dominant force in my life. How could God's grace or anything else every occupy a greater place than those many items? I thought she finished her part of the session, but Mrs. Julia added one final appeal before being seated:

> *"Marvelous, infinite, matchless grace, freely bestowed on all who believe; You that are longing to see His face, will you this moment His grace receive?"*[104]

I looked out of the corner of my eye and saw the person sitting on my left shaking his head "no." That distracted me from following the speaker. I looked again at the person and confirmed the Tempter occupying that seat with his devilish grin. How did he always show up to sit near me in such settings? Why did he always sit on my left? He never sat on the right side. He did not say a word to me, his distractive strategy proved successful. I was not yet longing to see the face of The Prince. As a matter of fact, had he appeared in the chapel I likely would have been greatly ashamed because all my luggage surely displeased Him.[105] I quickly reasoned that if I became one of His followers, I would have ample time to do so in the future. Two or three passengers seated nearby accepted His free grace at that moment and had their tickets stamped to go to Calvary when we reached that salvation station. Alas, I resisted that action.

One of the porters seemed to sense that some of us were struggling with this most important of all decisions. He arose and reminded the crowd that there is a difference between grace and mercy. He indicated that grace is The Conductor giving us what we do not deserve, and mercy is Him withholding from us, what we do deserve. Even though the theme of the chapel focused on grace, he did not want us to forget the marvel of God's mercy. With that in mind, he pulled out a cablegram from Charles Wesley that he sent to the train after he left us a few days ago. The message described a man who had said "no" to The Conductor too often and too loud:

"Depth of mercy! Can there be, mercy still reserved for me? Can my God His wrath forbear? Me, the chief of sinners spare.

I have long withstood His grace, long provoked Him to His face; Would not hearken to His calls, grieved Him by a thousand falls.

I my Master have denied, I afresh have crucified; Oft profaned His hallowed name, put Him to an open shame.

There for me the Savior stands, shows His wounds, and spreads His hands; God is love! I know, I feel, Jesus weeps, but loves me still.

Now incline me to repent, let me now my fall lament; Now my foul revolt deplore, weep, believe, and sin no more."[106]

The porter urged those who were in the "valley of decision" to listen intently to the last speaker, a Mr. E.O. Excell, who gave this testimony:

"In looking through my tears one day, I found Mount Calvary; Beneath the cross there flowed a stream of grace, enough for me.

While standing there my trembling heart once full of agony; Could scarce believe the sight I saw of grace, enough for me.

When I beheld my every sin, nailed to the cruel tree; I felt a flood go through my soul, of grace, enough for me.

When I am safe within the veil my portion there will be; To sing through all the years to come, of grace, enough for me."[107]

Those last two words "for me" pierced my soul like an arrow straight from the heavenly archers. A few minutes later I left the chapel service, but that chapel service did not leave me. My Companion met me again as I later ate alone in the Dining Car, rode alone in the Coach Car, and prepared to get some rest in the Sleeper Car. He somehow blended all the voices from the chapel with his own gentle tones to urge me to prepare for the coming stop at Calvary where I, too, could find "grace enough for me."

Chapter Five –

SUFFERING

The people that served The Prince experienced their share of heartache, suffering, and grief. The *Ecclesia Express* traveled through all kinds of weather and the storms of life battered cars that contained both the just and the unjust.[108] During one specific segment of the trip, it became clear that almost every passenger experienced some degree of hardship, whether physical, mental, spiritual, or financial. To address these concerns, the porters reserved the Lounge Car one evening for what they called a "Symposium on Suffering." I looked forward to attending because for years the existence of evil served as a stumbling block to any faith I could project toward The Conductor. The Tempter constantly captured my ear to whisper:

"If there is an almighty Conductor, why does He allow so much suffering? If He cannot do anything about it, then He is not all powerful and if He will not do anything about it, He certainly can't be a God of love."

I knew why good things happened to good people and why bad things happened to bad people. The laws of cause and effect verify that is the way things should be. The chapel on grace helped me begin to understand why good things happen to bad people. But the lingering question that I and some other passengers had is why do bad things happen to good people? Specifically, God's people – the followers of The Prince.

The night of the symposium arrived, and the Lounge Car underwent a transformation into a makeshift lecture hall. The porters, as always, prepared the audience with a pamphlet filled with pertinent passages from The Schedule.[109] The platform contained a table where a panel of a half dozen passengers sat. A couple of microphones were positioned in the audience for questions or comments. The place was packed with people and a porter began the event right on time. He soon introduced the first speaker, a gentleman named Frank Graeff. This man set the stage for the discussion:

"Does Jesus care when my heart is pained too deeply for mirth or song? As the burdens press and the cares distress, and the way grows weary and long.

Does Jesus care when my way is dark with a nameless dread and fear? As the daylight fades into deep night shades, does He care enough to be near?

Does Jesus care when I've tried and failed to resist some temptation strong? When for my deep grief there is no relief, though my tears flow all night long?

Does Jesus care when I've said 'good-bye' to the dearest on earth to me? And my sad heart aches till it nearly breaks, is it aught to Him, does He see?"[110]

After posing these questions the opening speaker folded up his notes and appeared to be finished. Then he suddenly raised his voice and declared without referring to his notes:

"Oh, yes, He cares, I know He cares, His heart is touched with my grief; When the days are weary, the long nights dreary, I know my Savior cares."[111]

I was not surprised that a passenger loyal to The Prince would assert such a positive testimony. But how could we know that for sure? That question lingered in my spirit. Before we heard from the panel, the porter in charge expressed delight that Aunt Fanny was in attendance, and he asked her to greet the audience and give a short word. Someone helped her to the microphone where she shared:

> *"All the way my Savior leads me, what have I to ask beside? Can I doubt His tender mercy, who through life has been my Guide?*
>
> *Heavenly peace, divinest comfort, here by faith in Him to dwell, For I know whate'er befall me, Jesus doeth all things well."*[112]

Leave it to Aunt Fanny to remind us that The Schedule affirms that the Judge of the Earth will always do right.[113] The porter recognized another lady in the audience who I did not know. I believe he identified her as Mrs. Frederick Suffield. She, too, went to the microphone and added this brief observation:

> *"God is still on the throne, and He will remember His own, though trials may press us and burdens distress us, He never will leave us alone;*
>
> *God is still on the throne, He never forsaketh His own, His promise is true, He will not forget you, God is still on the throne."*[114]

I did not know the person sitting next to me near the back of the Lounge Car. At that point he leaned over and whispered to me:

> *"I've seen the lightning flashing, and heard the thunder roll, I've felt sin's breakers dashing, trying to conquer my soul;*
>
> *I've heard the voice of my Savior, telling me still to fight on, He promised never to leave me, never to leave me alone."*[115]

This interruption startled me, but I smiled, nodded my head, and turned my attention back to the platform. The first designated speaker on the stage received introduction as Pastor William C. Martin. He was a close friend to Charles Gabriel, whom I had met at my first breakfast on the train. Pastor Martin proved to be a prolific communicator. I took note that he spoke about The Conductor and The Prince. Concerning the former, he proclaimed:

> *"I trust in God wherever I may be, upon the land or on the rolling sea; For come what may, from day to day, My heavenly Father watches over me.*
>
> *I trust in God, I know He cares for me, on mountain bleak or on the stormy sea; Though billows roll, He keeps the soul, my heavenly Father watches over me.*
>
> *"He makes the rose an object of His care, He guides the eagle through the pathless air; And surely He remembers me, My heavenly Father watches over me.*
>
> *I trust in God, for in the lion's den, on battlefield or in the prison pen; Through praise or blame, through flood or flame, My heavenly Father watches over me.*
>
> *The valley may be dark, the shadows deep, but oh the Shepherd guards His lonely sheep; And through the gloom He'll lead me home, My heavenly Father watches over me."*[116]

Those powerful points penetrated my spirit. I pondered that if his premise is true, the circumstances that surround us are irrelevant. Pastor Martin waxed equally eloquent when he gave his personal testimony about living for the Son of The Conductor, The Prince Himself:

> *"My heart is sometimes heavy, but He comes with sweet relief, He folds me to His bosom when I droop with blighting grief;*
>
> *I love the Christ who all my burdens in His body bore, each day He grows still sweeter than He was the day before."*[117]

The next panelist to greet the people stepped forth, a Mrs. Civilla Martin. (She was not related to the previous pastor.) She told of once visiting friends – a long time married couple who were both going through much physical suffering. Their exemplary spirit and attitude made a great impact upon her own life. She asked the crowd at the symposium these questions:

> *"Why should I feel discouraged, why should the shadows come, why should my heart be lonely and long for Heaven and home?*
>
> *When Jesus is my portion, my constant Friend is He, His eye is on the sparrow and I know He watches me.*
>
> *I sing because I'm happy, I sing because I'm free; For His eye is on the sparrow and I know He watches me."*[118]

She then directly spoke to any who might be presently experiencing a significant trial. Her words of encouragement included:

> *"Be not dismayed whate'er betide, God will take care of you; Beneath His wings of love abide, God will take care of you.*
>
> *Through days of toil when heart doth fail, God will take care of you; When dangers fierce your path assail, God will take care of you.*
>
> *God will take care of you, through every day, o'er all the way, He will take care of you, God will take care of you."*[119]

The porter then arose and affirmed what had already been shared. He pointed out to the audience the giant banner that Thomas Moore designed which hung over the entire stage. It read:

> *"Earth has no sorrow Heaven cannot heal."*[120]

I wrote that down as something worth remembering. The porter introduced four other panelists who briefly addressed the assembly before the discussion began.

First to speak came John Sammis. He shared this succinct saying:

> *"Trust and obey, for there's no other way, to be happy in Jesus, but to trust and obey.*

Not a burden we bear, not a sorrow we share, but our toil He doth richly repay; Not a grief or a loss, not a frown or a cross, but is blessed if we trust and obey."[121]

Louisa Stead, an ardent follower of The Prince, offered a presentation that emphasized the same theme:

"Tis so sweet to trust in Jesus, just to take Him at His Word; Just to rest upon His promise, just to know 'Thus saith the Lord.

Jesus, Jesus, how I trust Him, how I've proved Him o'er and o'er; Jesus, Jesus, precious Jesus, Oh for grace to trust Him more."[122]

She testified to proving The Prince in the past, trusting Him in the present, and depending on more of His grace for the future.

Joseph Gilmore followed the lady. He echoed many of the previous sentiments in his own unique way:

"He leadeth me, O blessed thought! O words with heavenly comfort fraught; Whate'er I do, where'er I be, still 'tis God's hand that leadeth me.

Sometimes 'mid scenes of deepest gloom, sometimes where Eden's bowers bloom; By waters still, o'er troubled sea, still 'tis His hand that leadeth me.

Lord, I would place my hand in Thine, nor ever murmur nor repine; Content, whatever lot I see, since 'tis my God that leadeth me

He leadeth me, He leadeth me, by His own hand He leadeth me; His faithful follower I would be, for by His hand He leadeth me."[123]

The fourth speaker, George Young, also talked about trusting the Lord in adversity:

"Sometimes on the mount where the sun shines so bright, God leads His dear children along; Sometimes in the valley, in darkest of night, God leads His dear children along.

Some through the waters, some through the flood, Some through the fire, but all through the blood; Some through great sorrow, but God gives a song, In the night season and all the day long."[124]

I found Mr. Young's report the most compelling of them all. No one can deny that throughout history, some received healing, and others did not. Some of the followers of The Prince were taken out of suffering and others were taken through it. The Schedule contained numerous examples of both.[125] This explains why in the early days of the train, one apostle was miraculously released from prison, while another remained in jail to be executed. [126]

The six guests on the platform continued with a discussion of the subject, then they took some questions from the audience. The porter came back and announced that we would be taking a short break. After the intermission, he indicated we would be privy to hearing some powerful testimonies from those who overcame great sorrow. I looked forward to the second session. I did not mingle with others during the break. The only person I spoke with was a young man named Ira, who sat in front of me during the first half of the symposium. We both agreed the first half was good, perhaps more informational than inspirational. Before Ira stepped out into the corridor during the break, he shared this simple secret.

"I know who holds tomorrow."[127]

I often heard that no one knows what tomorrow holds. What a comforting thought that we could know the One who holds tomorrow!

I thanked Ira for sharing that insight as I sat back down in my seat. I had not yet taken the time to read the program that the porters had handed to us when we arrived. On the back cover was an illustration of trusting The Conductor that several of the speakers alluded to. The artist provided her signature, Florence Alt, at the bottom of her literary masterpiece:

"My life is but a weaving between my God and me, I cannot choose the colors He worketh steadily;

Sometimes He weaveth sorrow, and I in foolish pride, Forget He sees the upper, and I the under-side

Not till the loom is silent and the shuttles cease to fly, Shall God unroll the canvas and explain the reason why;

The dark threads are as needful in the Weaver's skillful hand, as the threads of gold and silver, in the pattern He has planned.

My life is but a weaving between my God and me, I see the seams, the tangles, but He sees perfectly;

He knows, He loves, He cares, nothing this truth can dim, He gives His very best to those who choose to walk with Him."[128]

My mind drifted deep into that imagery until I heard the porter's voice calling the symposium back to order. For the second half of the event, the table on the stage had been removed and the previous panelists took their seats in the audience. The porter introduced the first testifier to the faithfulness of The Conductor. His name was Horatio Spafford. This renowned lawyer also served as an elder in the church. He faced unimaginable grief after four daughters perished at sea in a transatlantic voyage in which only his wife survived. The Lounge Car came to a noticeable hush in anticipation of what he would say. Finally, the silence was shattered:

"When peace like a river attended my way, when sorrows like sea billows rolled; Whatever my lot, Thou hast taught me to say, 'It is well, It is well with my soul."[129]

There was not a dry eye in the assembly when he repeated:

"It is well, it is well, with my soul."

First one, and then another, then eventually the entire delegation present chanted softly with him:

"It is well with my soul."

After the distinguished lawyer spoke for several more minutes, the porter introduced the second guest. This gentleman bore the name of Luther Bridgers. He was an evangelist in the southern part of his country. He too had experienced similar heartache to Mr. Spafford. While he was engaged in traveling and sharing the good news of The Schedule from place to place, his wife and children perished in a tragic house fire. When he approached the microphone, suspense increased as to what he would say in this setting. He delivered this testimony:

> *"All my life was wrecked by sin and strife, discord filled my heart with pain; Jesus swept across the broken strings, stirred the slumbering cords again.*
>
> *Jesus, Jesus, Jesus, sweetest name I know; Fills my every longing, keeps me singing as I go."*[130]

The audience again felt touched by his resilient faith and trust in The Prince. I marveled that these men demonstrated no anger or bitterness toward The Conductor. Rather, they too found a place of assurance and hope, even when their world was shaking to the core. The third and final testifier also knew supreme grief and sorrow. The porter introduced him as Mr. Thomas A. Dorsey. His wife died giving birth to their child, who also did not survive. Mr. Dorsey's words touched everyone in the place as he shared how he prayed to The Prince:

> *"Take my hand, Precious Lord."*[131]

It seemed obvious that his grief persisted and his reliance on The Prince for daily help continued in the present tense. Others may have shared at the symposium, but I left shortly after these three speakers. I heard enough to have learned a couple of things. First, being a follower of The Prince does not exempt a person from problems, plights, and pain. In fact, sometimes those in The Conductor's family seem to suffer more in this life than those who are not related to Him. The Prince previously told that ancient apostle that very thing after his conversion.[132] Second, the suffering saints of The Prince are given sufficient grace to endure trials and tribulations.[133]

That second truth I learned received confirmation the next morning in a conversation with a person named Annie J. Flint. She was a twice-or-phaned woman who suffered for decades, requiring the care of others. She too attended the symposium and we exchanged notes we had made while we traveled in the Coach Car together. I noticed she had also been present at the Lord's Day Chapel on grace, however, she did not speak during that session. On this occasion, she succinctly summarized what several of the speakers discussed about overcoming adversity in their lives:

> *"He giveth more grace when the burdens grow greater, He sendeth more strength when the labors increase; To added afflictions He addeth His mercy, to multiplied trials, His multiplied* peace.
>
> *When we have exhausted our store of endurance, when our strength has failed ere the day is half done; When we reach the end of our hoarded resources, our Father's full giving is only begun.*
>
> *His love has no limits, His grace has no measure, His power no boundary known unto men; For out of His infinite riches in Jesus, He giveth and giveth and giveth again."*[134]

She no sooner finished her eloquent speech when suddenly a man walking in the aisle through the car stopped and turned around to face us. We both appeared surprised to see John Newton standing there. He heard Annie Flint's language about grace and felt impressed to add another thought on the subject:

> *"Through many dangers, toils and snares, I have already come, It was grace that brought me safe this far, and grace will lead me home."*[135]

I remembered a porter standing in the middle of the Chapel Car once while pointing to the left wall, saying,

"I used to be over there and now I'm standing here. I am on my way over there (pointing to the right wall)."

People ask me,

"How are you going to make it there?"

"The same thing that brought me from there to here will lead me all the way there too!"

The third truth I gleaned from the symposium is that we will not have all the questions like "why?" "why me?" "why us?" "why not?" and "why now?" answered in this life. I arrived at this conclusion via a chance conversation later that afternoon. I stepped out on the caboose to catch a breath of fresh air. Two gentlemen were engaged in a discussion. I did not want to crowd them, so I said: "Excuse me" and turned to go back into the train. However, when I heard the subject of their conversation, I intentionally lingered with my hand on the door long enough to hear part of their verbal exchange. I believe one man's last name was Stevens. I heard him say:

> "Tempted and tried, we're oft made to wonder, why it should be thus all the day long; While there are others living about us, never molested, though in the wrong.
>
> Farther along we'll know more about it, farther along we'll understand why; Cheer up my brother, live in the sunshine, We'll understand it all by and by."[136]

I knew the second man. Almost everyone on the train likely knew Mr. Charles Tindley. He picked up on what Mr. Stevens said and delivered this reply:

> "Trials dark on every hand and we cannot understand all the ways that God would lead us to that blessed promised land; But He'll guide us with His eye, and we'll follow till we die, we will understand it better by and by.

By and by when the morning comes, when all the saints of God are gathered home; We will tell the story how we've overcome, and we'll understand it better by and by."[137]

I turned my head to take a quick glance at the many miles we had already traveled. I knew much more than I did when I boarded the train, but like the countless miles ahead, so much more remained for me to learn.

Chapter Six –

THE CROSS

To no one's surprise, the sign at the Chapel Car revealed "The Cross" as the theme of the next Lord's Day Chapel. After all, we were getting closer to Calvary, the main hub on this railway system designed by The Conductor to transport passengers to the Shining City. My Companion informed me of this before I boarded the train and all the porters often repeated that no other route existed to that majestic destination. For those who did not stop at Calvary they would be placed on a different train heading in the opposite direction from the Shining City. It made sense that the last chapel before that important train stop would focus on the death of The Prince on the cross.

I considered not attending this chapel for two reasons. First, just the gruesome execution itself became something I tried to block from my mind. Second, I knew the discussion would likely focus on sin. I did not need a reminder of the many boxes, packages, and bags that I had hoarded in my berth in the Sleeping Car. I both loved and hated those sins at the same time. I realized I could never take that luggage into the Shining City and that I would have to leave them at Calvary if I wanted to go all the way on this train. With all that stirring in my spirit I decided at the last minute to attend. I went into the chapel service just before it began. One of the passengers, John Bowring, had hung a large banner over the front of the chapel that read:

"In the cross of Christ I glory, towering o'er the wrecks of time."[138]

I found my favorite seat empty on the back row, and I quietly slipped into it. It did not take long for my heart to be convicted. The distinguished Isaac Watts broke the silence with the opening address. I met him earlier on the caboose shortly after beginning my trip, I heard him at the Christmas service, and now he was challenging us all with his inspired rhetoric:

"When I survey the wondrous cross, on which the Prince of glory died, my richest gain I count but loss, and pour contempt on all my pride.

Forbid it, Lord, that I should boast, save in the death of Christ my God; All the vain things that charm me most, I sacrifice them to His blood.

See from His head, His hands, His feet, sorrow and love flow mingled down; Did e'er such love and sorrow meet, or thorns compose so rich a crown?

Were the whole realm of nature mine, that were a present far too small; Love so amazing, so divine, demands my soul, my life, my all."[139]

How could someone who did not know me speak so directly as if he were reading my mind and surveying my soul? If The Prince had paid the ultimate price for me, would I be willing to pay the cost of what following Him demanded? A minister from the Midwest by the name of George Bennard went to the lectern next. His task consisted of describing the setting on that most monumental day in human history. Here is how he did it:

"On a hill far away stood an old rugged cross, the emblem of suffering and shame; And I love that old cross where the Dearest and Best, for a world of lost sinners was slain.

Oh, that old rugged cross, so despised by the world, has a wondrous attraction for me; For the dear Lamb of God left His glory above, to bear it to dark Calvary.

In that old rugged cross, stained with blood so divine, a wondrous beauty I see; For 'twas on that old cross, Jesus suffered and died, to pardon and sanctify me.

So I'll cherish the old rugged cross, till my trophies at last I lay down; I will cling to the old rugged cross and exchange it someday for a crown."[140]

As Bennard continued to speak, I contemplated how he or anyone could "love that old cross" and find in it a "wondrous attraction" or a "wondrous beauty." And then it struck me. Just as I professed to both love and hate my baggage at the same time, so too could the followers of The Prince both love their Savior for dying in such a way for them, while at the same time hating the suffering that their sins and human soldiers inflicted upon Him.

Isaac Watts must have been appointed in charge of the chapel service because he returned to the platform and challenged the crowd with a question:

"Am I a soldier of the cross, a follower of the Lamb, and shall I fear to own His cause, or blush to speak His name?[141]

He continued to admonish those present to make certain that we got off the train when we stopped at Calvary. He then pulled out a couple of cablegrams to read from recent passengers on the *Ecclesia Express.* These provided additional exhortations to have our tickets stamped for the Calvary stop. The first message was from a Mr. Moody. His instructions were very clear:

"Kneel at the cross, Christ will meet you there, come while He waits for you; List to His voice, leave with Him your care, and begin life anew.

Kneel at the cross, there is room for all, who would His glory share; Bliss there awaits, harm can ne'er befall, those who are anchored there.

Kneel at the cross, give your idols up, Look unto realms above; Turn not away, to life's sparkling cup, Trust only in His love."[142]

"Give your idols up!" Those words pierced me like an arrow. I was getting the point (sharply) that I could not have my sins and a Savior at the same time. The second cablegram was concise. It was penned by a Mr. Ogden. Although brief, it contained a large quantity of hope:

"I've a message from the Lord, hallelujah! This message unto you I'll give; 'Tis recorded in His Word, hallelujah! It is only that you 'look and live.'

'Look and live,' my brother, live, Look to Jesus now and live; 'Tis recorded in His Word, hallelujah! It is only that you 'look and live."[143]

The porters stressed to us that this is what the stop at Calvary meant. They said to look trustingly upon the Lamb on the cross produces life for those who are drawn to Him.[144]

Isaac Watts then pointed us to the bulletin that had been provided to us for this service. I had already noticed the words composed by Jessie Pounds on the back cover:

"I must needs go home by the way of the cross, there's no other way but this; I shall never get sight of the gates of light, if the way of the cross I miss.

I must needs go on in the blood-sprinkled way, the path that the Savior trod; If I ever climb to the heights sublime, where the soul is at home with God.

Then I bid farewell to the way of the world, to walk in it nevermore; For my Lord says 'Come" and I seek my home, where He waits at the open door."[145]

As Watts instructed, we opened our bulletins to find the printed agenda for this service. He brought our attention to the program now calling for testimonies from people who had already made the life changing stop at Calvary. A gentleman named S.J. Henderson went first. He excitedly proclaimed:

> *"Saved by the blood of the Crucified One! Now ransomed from sin and a new work begun.*
>
> *Sing praise to the Father and praise to the Son, Saved by the blood of the Crucified One.*
>
> *Saved by the blood of the Crucified One! The angels rejoicing because it is done; A child of the Father, joint-heir with the Son, Saved by the blood of the Crucified One.*
>
> *Saved by the blood of the Crucified One! The Father He spake and His will it was done; Great price of my pardon, His own precious Son, Saved by the blood of the Crucified One.*
>
> *Glory, I'm saved! Glory, I'm saved! My sins are all pardoned, my guilt is all gone! Glory, I'm saved! Glory, I'm saved! I'm saved by the blood of the Crucified One."*[146]

That powerful testimony paved the way for William Cowper. I heard rumors this man had overcome many obstacles, including spending time in a sanatorium. I leaned up on the edge of my seat to hear what he might say about The Prince, the Cross, and Calvary. He spoke with deep conviction these remarks:

> *"There is a fountain filled with blood, drawn from Immanuel's veins; And sinners plunged beneath that flood, lose all their guilty stains.*
>
> *The dying thief rejoiced to see that fountain in his day; And there have I, though vile as he, washed all my sins away.*
>
> *Ever since by faith I saw the stream, Thy flowing wounds supply; Redeeming love has been my theme and shall be till I die."*[147]

I recalled reading in The Schedule about that dying thief who called The Prince on the middle tree "Lord" on that fateful day at Calvary.[148] The Prince erased all attempts to ever question that His mercy endures forever when He promised passage to the Shining City to that dying criminal. I had to admit inwardly that these were two amazing transformations – a doomed thief with only a few breaths left in his body and a troubled man now able to speak with such eloquence. A woman was next in the printed order, and everyone seemed to listen more intently when this Mrs. Taylor spoke. She talked about her past, which included sin, shame, guilt, and despair, before triumphantly proclaiming,

"Calvary covers it all."[149]

Whoever arranged for these speakers could not have found better ambassadors to make the case for stopping at the cross. Another woman, whose first name was Avis, also addressed the chapel. She spoke in such a way that it almost seemed we were back in time at the very moment when the crucifixion of The Prince took place:

"Up Calvary's mountain, one dreadful morn, walked Christ my Savior, weary and worn; Facing for sinners death on the cross, that He might save them from endless loss.

Blessed Redeemer! Precious Redeemer! Seems now I see Him on Calvary's tree; Wounded and bleeding, for sinners pleading, blind and unheeding – dying for me.

Oh, how I love Him, Savior and Friend, how can my praises ever find end; Through years unnumbered on Heaven's shore, my tongue shall praise Him forevermore."[150]

By the time she finished her dialogue, several in the chapel were shouting "amen" and nodding their heads in agreement. Only two more names remained listed in the program to speak. Isaac Watts returned to the podium. He invited Mr. William Newell to come and address the crowd. While this gentleman was coming to the front, Watts reminded us that the train would be arriving at the Calvary station in just a few days. He indicated that porters were present and would be available after the chapel to stamp the tickets of those who planned on stopping there for the first time. Part of me wanted to commit to going at that very moment, however, I also remained torn, still thinking about all my luggage and the contents which I had gathered over a lifetime. Isaac Watts then concluded his introduction of Mr. Newell, saying he was coming to tell us what to expect at Calvary. Mr. Newell certainly did that:

> "*Years I spent in vanity and pride, caring not my Lord was crucified; Knowing not it was for me He died, on Calvary.*
>
> *Mercy there was great. and grace was free, Pardon there was multiplied to me; There my burdened soul found liberty, at Calvary.*
>
> *By God's Word at last my sin I learned, then I trembled at the law I'd spurned; Till my guilty soul imploring turned to Calvary.*
>
> *Now I've given to Jesus everything, now I gladly own Him as my King; Now my raptured soul can only sing, of Calvary.*
>
> *Oh, the love that drew salvation's plan, Oh, the grace that brought it down to man; Oh, the mighty gulf that God did span at Calvary.*"[151]

I had never heard such magnificent words uttered by human lips before. How could I possibly comprehend all that Mr. Newell had experienced on his journey to the place where The Prince died in his stead? "Vanity" and "Pride" not only had been my lifelong companions, they also remained the chief sins recorded against my name. I, too, lived as if I did not care that The Prince had been executed for me. My guilt felt heavier than ever before. I sensed that I had not only broke The Conductor's laws; I had also broken His heart. My burdened soul longed for liberty, but not yet to the point of having my ticket stamped for Calvary. Oh, how torn between two lifestyles I became!

Evidently, I was not the only one moved by his speech. Isaac Watts prepared to introduce the last speaker on the program, but instead he spontaneously shared more about his own experience at Calvary:

"At the cross, at the cross, where I first saw the light, and the burden of my heart rolled away; It was there by faith I received my sight, and now I am happy all the day.

Alas and did my Savior bleed and did my Sovereign die? Would He devote that sacred head for such a worm as I?

Was it for crimes that I had done, He groaned upon the tree? Amazing pity, grace unknown, and love beyond degree.

Well might the sun in darkness hide and shut his glories in, when God the mighty maker died for man, the creature's sin.

The drops of grief can ne'er repay the debt of love I owe; Dear Lord, I give myself away, 'tis all that I can do."[152]

His words met with great affirmation among those seated around me. The more these people talked, the more conscious I became about my own burden of sin. My bags were not just filled with trinkets of this world, they were packed with shame, guilt, and an ever-growing realization that my selfishness caused the perfect sinless Prince to come and die for.[153] What condescension! The Prince dying for the pauper! The Mighty Maker dying for the miserable masses! The Sacred Head wounded for sinful humanity's wickedness! I felt as if I could not tolerate another minute more. Suddenly, I noticed the Tempter had slipped into the meeting and was occupying the empty chair next to me. He leaned over and began to whisper that all this was nonsense – a made up religious story to enslave weak minded and uneducated people. He reminded me how good that I was and that most people looked up to me. He laughed when they spoke about sin and mocked The Prince for being so weak, He allowed Himself to die such a shameful death. He chatted so much I could no longer hear Isaac Watts clearly. Rather than try to force him to leave me alone, I stood up and walked to the door of the chapel. I decided to go ahead and leave the room, but at that moment the last speaker was introduced, a Mr. John Moore. I stopped near the exit and listened to his closing remarks. He repeatedly shouted:

"Burdens are lifted at Calvary."[154]

At one point John Moore used the term, "Troubled soul" and I felt he was pointing right at me. It seemed every speaker had mentioned burdens and every time they did, I thought of all the treasures I had accumulated in those bags on my bed in the Sleeper Car. I felt like a civil war broke out in my heart with both sides shooting at me.[155] When I was away from him, I knew the Tempter lurked as a scoundrel who should not be trusted. Yet his words always appealed to those lower urges that long had dominated my life. His voice always contradicted My Companion who had convinced me to get on this train and set out for the Shining City. When My Companion spoke, it always resonated within me as being the truth. The Tempter's voice sounded like privilege – do what you want to do. My Companion's voice sounded like principle – do what you should do. These passengers who praised The Prince had something I did not have, and I confess, I secretly longed for. Their lives seemed to match their message and part of me wanted to trade all my luggage for the joy that filled their existence.

I felt I could not breathe anymore so I stepped out of the chapel into the corridor. One of the porters that I became friends with came and placed his arm around me. He could see that I had been wiping away tears for the last several minutes. He asked me if I was ready to have him stamp my ticket for the stop at Calvary, now scheduled just a few days away. I thought for a moment I would do it. I even reached into my pocket and pulled my ticket out. But then I heard myself saying,

"Not yet, I have some things I need to do first."

We talked for a few more moments and then I excused myself and walked back to my berth in the Sleeping Car. As I was walking away, Ira, the gentleman I had met at the suffering symposium saw me and cried from afar:

"There's room at the cross for you."[156]

It seemed I heard him say it again and again. A porter confirmed that it is never too crowded at the cross. That night, lying in bed with my baggage all around me, Ira's words were the last thing I heard over and over in my head until finally I went to sleep.

Chapter Seven –

THE RESURRECTION

The chapel highlighting the cross dominated my mind for the next two days. I could not escape the words I heard and the images that I saw concerning the death of The Prince. The next day, I joined two other people in the Lounge Car to discuss some business matters. While we met there, three other men approached us. Each of them had some questions they proceeded to ask. The first gentleman I knew as Reverend Lowry. He asked and then answered the first questions:

> *"What can wash away my sin? Nothing but the blood of Jesus. What can make me whole again? Nothing but the blood of Jesus.*
>
> *Oh, precious is the flow, that makes me white as snow; No other Fount I know, nothing but the blood of Jesus."*[157]

Everyone on the train knew the second man. Elisha Hoffman long ago hung the giant banner that stretched out over the Lounge Car. He too asked a series of questions to us:

"Have you been to Jesus for the cleansing power, are you washed in the blood of the Lamb? Are you fully trusting in His grace this hour? Are you washed in the blood of the Lamb?

Are you washed in the blood? In the soul cleansing blood of the Lamb? Are your garments spotless, are they white as snow? Are you washed in the blood of the Lamb?

Are you walking daily by the Savior's side? Are you washed in the blood of the Lamb? Do you rest each moment in the Crucified? Are you washed in the blood of the Lamb?

When the Bridegroom cometh will your robes be white? Pure and white in the blood of the Lamb?

Will your soul be ready for the mansions bright, and be washed in the blood of the Lamb?"[158]

Before anyone could respond to those questions, the third man, a Mr. Lewis Jones, peppered us with another set of his own:

"Would you be free from your burden of sin? There's power in the blood, power in the blood. Would you o'er evil a victory win? There's wonderful power in the blood.

Would you be free from your passion and pride? There's power in the blood, power in the blood. Come for a cleansing to Calvary's tide, There's wonderful power in the blood.

Would you be whiter, much whiter than snow? There's power in the blood, power in the blood. Sin stains are lost in its life giving flow, There's wonderful power in the blood.

Would you do service for Jesus, your King? There's power in the blood, power in the blood. Would you live daily His praises to sing? There's wonderful power in the blood."[159]

My mind became dizzy trying to sort out those twenty questions. I did not know where to begin to try to answer them. Thankfully, the two passengers meeting with me spoke up first. Mrs. Anna Waterman answered them directly:

"And I know, yes, I know, Jesus' blood can make the vilest sinner clean;
And I know, yes I know, Jesus' blood can make the vilest sinner clean."[160]

Her emphatic reply sounded so affirming! She proceeded to tell the gentlemen that she remained active in seeking to lead others to the cross. She knew her message well:

"Come ye sinners, lost and hopeless, Jesus' blood can make you free;
For He saved the worst among you, when He saved a wretch like me."[161]

The other gentleman we were visiting with, E.M. Bartlett, smiled during all the questions and the reply from Anna Waterman. Someone asked him why and he simply replied:

"Victory in Jesus."[162]

Mr. Bartlett went on to explain why he loved The Prince and why he wanted to reach the Shining City:

"There we'll meet the One who saved us and who kept us by His grace,
and who brought us to that land so bright and fair; We will praise His
name forever as we look upon His face, Everybody will be happy over
there."[163]

The three questioners seemed pleased with both replies. I thought they would all expect my response next. Somehow the conversation shifted and soon they were all discussing other traits of The Prince. I found a way to discreetly dismiss myself from the group and I vacated the scene. Right before I left the Lounge Car, a young man named Andre stopped me at the door. He evidently sat near our table and heard the conversation with the questioners. He told me he knew something about the shed blood of The Prince that the others did not mention. I asked him to tell me, and he answered:

"The blood will never lose its power."[164]

I smiled, shook his hand, thanked him, and slipped away. The next day I stepped out on to the caboose for some fresh air. The missionary, Stuart Hine, and the lawyer, H.G. Spafford, filled the air with a pleasant conversation about how close we were to Calvary. I turned to go back into the Coach Car, however, they both asked me to join them for a short time. I accepted their request. As their discussion continued, I asked them what they perceived to be the greatest benefit a person could derive by getting off the train at Calvary. Hine answered first:

"And when I think that God, His Son not sparing, sent Him to die, I scarce can take it in; That on the cross, my burden gladly bearing, He bled and died to take away my sin."[165]

I felt unprepared for such a powerful response. When I posed the same question to the lawyer, he delivered an equally passionate come back:

"My sin – Oh, the bliss of this glorious thought, my sin, not in part, but the whole; Is nailed to the cross and I bear it no more, Praise the Lord, Praise the Lord, Oh my soul."[166]

Why did the tears keep coming into my eyes? How could my heart receive so many arrows from the archers of The Prince? I felt My Companion arranged this impromptu meeting on the caboose. The testimonies of sins being forgiven kept piling up from highly credible people.

Likewise, those questions from the three gentlemen in the Lounge Car continued to rise to the forefront of my memory. I realized a decision loomed on whether I would exit the train when it stopped at Calvary. No one could deny that The Conductor sending His Son, The Prince, to die for a fallen race is the greatest love story in human comprehension – if it were indeed true. And the only way to prove the veracity of the account is if The Prince did not stay dead. On this third day after the cross chapel, I began to grapple with this very question.[167] As the train raced down the track, I got up and walked into the corridor before daybreak. I heard a voice coming from the adjacent Coach Car. It sounded like "Hallelujah." That word frequently found expression on the train, but in the wee hours of the morning my curiosity suddenly sparked. When I opened the door to the car, I could see a shadowy figure at the far end standing in the aisle. Whether it was a man or a woman I could not see. This person never saw me, but spoke these words into the dark air:

> "*The strife is o'er, the battle done; the victory of life is won; The song of triumph has begun: Alleluia!*
>
> *The powers of death have done their worst; but Christ their legions has dispersed; let shouts of holy joy outburst: Alleluia!*
>
> *The three sad days are quickly sped; He rises glorious from the dead; all glory to our risen Head: Alleluia!*
>
> *He closed the yawning gates of hell; the bars from heaven's high portals fell; let hymns of praise His triumphs tell: Alleluia!*
>
> *Lord, by the stripes which wounded You, in us you've won the victory too; that we may live and sing to You: Alleluia!*"[168]

This time I did not approach the speaker to initiate a conversation. I simply retreated and quietly closed the door to that Coach Car. The anonymous voice obviously spoke about the resurrection event. No wonder "alleluias" rang out. If indeed this happened, it surely must qualify as the greatest of all miracles. As a matter of fact, I began to reason within myself. Either The Prince arose from the dead, or He did not. If He did not, I am wise for remaining outside of the faith. But if He did, one would be a fool to not embrace Him as Lord. If the bodily resurrection of The Prince did not happen, then no one should believe a single thing recorded in The Schedule. However, if it did occur, everything in The Schedule could be believed!

I pondered the ramifications of the resurrection claim through most of the morning. Shortly after noon I ventured to the Dining Car to eat lunch. I selected a small table in the corner and fully expected to dine alone with all these thoughts rushing through my head. A few minutes later, to my surprise, Reverend Lowry, with his tray of food in hand, asked if he could join me. He was one of the three men who challenged me with an array of questions that I still had not yet answered. He asked it again,

"What can wash away my sin?"

I gave a blank stare as he answered his own inquiry with,

"Nothing but the blood of Jesus."

One thing led to another and soon the conversation had transitioned to the story of the resurrection of The Prince. This time, I asked him the question,

"What do you think really happened on that long ago Sunday morning outside of Jerusalem?"

His eyes grew big with wonder, and he began to answer very slowly:

"Low in the grave He lay, Jesus, my Savior, Waiting the coming day, Jesus, my Lord.

Vainly they watch His bed, Jesus, my Savior, Vainly they seal the dead, Jesus, my Lord.

Death cannot keep his Prey, Jesus, my Savior, He tore the bars away, Jesus, my Lord."[169]

Suddenly, Revered Lowry's voice began to crescendo with excitement as he slammed his hand on the table and shouted aloud:

"Up from the grave He arose, with a mighty triumph o'er His foes, He arose a Victor from the dark domain, and He lives forever with His saints to reign.

He arose! He arose! Hallelujah! Christ arose!"[170]

By this time, several people from surrounding tables had heard his declaration. Many of them were smiling, nodding their heads, or applauding his statement. No doubts filled the Reverend's mind, and no indecision came from his voice. At that moment, I wished I possessed his certainty about this miracle claim of all miracles. I wanted it to be true, but how could it be so, and we be so sure? The Reverend then appeared to think of something, and he asked me if I had met Charles Wesley when he rode with us on part of the journey some days ago. I replied that I never met him, but I did hear him talking to The Conductor once in the Communication Car and at the Christmas gathering. Reverend Lowry said that he himself had met Mr. Wesley during those days and the two of them had extended conversations together. He added that Wesley had sent him a cablegram that he had received that morning. He pulled it out of his pocket and proceeded to read part of it to me:

> "*Christ the Lord is risen today, Alleluia! Sons of men and angels say, Alleluia! Raise your joys and triumphs high, Alleluia! Sing, ye heavens and earth reply, Alleluia!*
>
> *Lives again our glorious King, Alleluia! Where, O death, is now thy sting? Alleluia! Once He died our souls to save, Alleluia! Where thy victory, O grave? Alleluia!*
>
> *Love's redeeming work is done, Alleluia! Fought the fight, the battle won, Alleluia! Death in vain forbids His rise, Alleluia! Christ has opened paradise, Alleluia!*
>
> *Soar we now where Christ hath led, Alleluia! Following our exalted Head, Alleluia! Made like Him, like Him we rise, Alleluia! Ours the cross, the grave, the skies, Alleluia!*"[171]

Hearing the cablegram from Charles Wesley reminded me of the mysterious voice I heard before dawn in the Coach Car that sounded out similar "hallelujahs" at the news of The Risen Prince. Wesley's words expressed something I had missed. Our own future resurrection is tied in directly with His glorious resurrection. If He did not rise, nor will we. But if He did, then our future living beyond the grave is an accomplished reality already. Reverend Lowry stayed another half hour or so, reminding me that the ancient apostle explained all of this in The Schedule to a Corinthian congregation that evidently felt as confused as I did.[172] What I presumed would be a quiet meal alone with my thoughts became a most rewarding and enjoyable discussion with a preacher who cared enough to spend some of his own valuable time with me.

That night one of the porters introduced me to a Mr. Charles Austin Miles. Like me, this gentleman had been reading the resurrection accounts in The Schedule.[173] He asked me to imagine what that first woman at the tomb must have felt when she saw the Risen Prince.

> *"I come to the garden alone, while the dew is still on the roses; And the voice I hear falling on my ear, the Son of God discloses…And He walks with me and He talks with me and He tells me I am His own; And the joy we share as we tarry there, none other has ever known."*[174]

The porter added that we all may experience such an encounter with the Prince of Life!

The next day I received a note from one of the porters that a prominent man named Mr. Ackley wanted to visit with me in the Lounge Car. I still do not know if Reverend Lowry had told him about me or how exactly he knew who I was. He was known to be proficient in communicating the message of The Risen Prince with others. After we exchanged common courtesy greetings, I asked him specifically why he believed in the resurrection of Christ and how he could be so sure. He listed many reasons before stating this conclusion:

> *"I serve a risen Savior, He's in the world today, I know that He is living, whatever men may say; I see His hand of mercy, I hear His voice of cheer, and just the time I need Him, He's always near…He lives! He lives! Christ Jesus lives today, He walks with me and talks with me*

along life's narrow way; He lives! He lives! Salvation to impart, You ask me how I know He lives? He lives within my heart."[175]

Like the other followers of The Prince that I spoke with, Mr. Ackley possessed great passion about his relationship with Christ. I certainly did not question nor dispute his claims. Those who had this testimony all contended that The Prince could not be dead because they had already conversed with Him that morning. Further evidence of The Risen Prince could be seen in the lives of His followers as they began to reflect His character and conduct. Yet I knew that the teaching of Christians was not just that He continued to live within the lives of believers in a spiritual way. On the contrary, the saints aboard the *Ecclesia Express* maintained that The Prince experienced a *bodily* resurrection by being raised to immortality.[176] After a brief conversation with Mr. Ackley, I thanked him and excused myself. I walked through the train until I found a Coach Car that appeared temporarily empty. I sat down in one of the seats near a window where I could look out while contemplating all the facts of the case. Perhaps I was too analytical, but I even found a pencil and notebook so I could arrange the data accordingly to address the resurrection question.

The tomb was empty on Sunday. Of that fact no debate exists. That does not in itself prove that Jesus arose. It only confirms the missing body. If The Prince did not rise again, someone must have taken His corpse. Who could or would have done that? The Romans? The Jews? What would be the purpose? Why would the Romans steal His body? They already had it. (I kept writing down all these things.) The Romans stationed guards so nothing would happen to Christ's body. If His enemies had the body, all they had to do at any moment in history is simply produce it and Christianity would have ended. (But the corpse was never produced because they did not have it!) Who else could have taken Him? The disciples? That is most incredulous of all! Where were they on Saturday? Hiding in some room behind locked doors. They were all filled with fear, guilt, and shame. Is it possible that one of them could suggest a plan to overpower armed guards, dispose of the body and then spend the rest of their lives traveling around the world telling people He was alive? How did the twelve apostles die? Almost all of them perished by brutal vicious deaths. Who would die for a lie? They would not be dying for something they thought was true; they would be dying for something they knew was false? (I wrote all these things down.) When I examined my list, the best evidence for the tomb being empty on Sunday morning is the resurrection of The Crown Prince! It takes more faith to believe something else than to believe this. Like the first apostle to reach the tomb that morn, I also observed the evidence, and even as he, believed.[177]

The next day I heard a group of men discussing this subject and especially Mr. Ackley's assertion that The Prince lives. A skeptic in the group posed the question – "He lives" – so what? What does that have to do with my life today? While the room grew silent and several did not know how to respond, a young man named Bill answered with one word: "Because."

I heard him say:

"Because He lives..."[178]

He proceeded to list several reasons why the resurrection is important. Not only does it provide pardon for our past and peace for our present, but the living Prince also vanquishes fear from our future. The convincing closing argument came from a prominent retired minister from another land. Pastor Oswald Smith said it this way:

"Their hearts were sad as in the tomb they laid Him, for death had come and taken Him away; Their night was dark and bitter tears were falling, then Jesus came and night was turned to day.

When Jesus comes, the tempter's power is broken, When Jesus comes, the tears are wiped away; He takes the gloom and fills the life with glory, for all is changed when Jesus comes to stay."[179]

The Risen Prince caused the Tempter to flee. Countless passengers aboard the *Ecclesia Express* exchanged their gloom for His glory! I had not yet confessed with my mouth the Lord Jesus, but I now believed in my heart that The Conductor had raised His Son from the dead. I now felt halfway home and knew I could not stay in that place very long. The most important decision of my life loomed just ahead.

Chapter Eight –

THE DECISION

T he train soon reached a pivotal place along the tracks. Calvary awaited as the next stop according to The Schedule. All passengers who had never been to that place received a summons to the Lounge Car for a special session together. Time became more valuable as the important choice drew near. We all had embarked on this trip knowing the "moment of truth" would eventually be at hand. All those who would go to Calvary for salvation would be allowed to re-enter the train to head on to the Shining City. However, those who refused to make the stop at this location would be placed on a train heading in the opposite direction. Astoundingly, The Prince once spoke that "many" would choose the latter, while only a "few" would select the former option.[180] This gathering in the Lounge Car provided one final invitation for us to consider before the whistle blew for the stop.

When we were all seated, the session began. A man named William J. Kilpatrick played a brief melody on a small piano to bring the meeting to order. A young woman, Priscilla Owens, stepped forth and shared the good news as clearly as it could be uttered:

"We have heard the joyful sound: Jesus saves! Jesus saves! Spread the tidings all around: Jesus saves! Jesus saves!

Bear the news to every land, climb the mountains, cross the waves, Onward! 'tis our Lord's command; Jesus saves! Jesus saves!"[181]

The issue to me became clearer. Jesus, The Crown Prince of Calvary indeed reigned as the Savior of the world. Would I allow Him to become my Savior? He had rescued so many mentioned in The Schedule and more traveling on this very train. Did I want to be rescued? Would I let Him rescue me? My Companion was present – constantly nudging me toward The Prince. The Tempter also lurked in the Lounge Car. I saw him darting in between unsuspecting passengers, telling them and me that we could decide this later and that I certainly did not have to surrender my vast collection of baggage that I had acquired. After the opening remarks, three people were lined up to rapidly provide their personal testimony. I found myself captivated by the words that each of them spoke. Mrs. Lelia Morris went first:

"In fancy I stood by the shore one day, of the beautiful murmuring sea, I saw the great crowds as they thronged the way, of the Stranger of Galilee.

I saw how the man who was blind from birth, in a moment was made to see; The lame was made whole by the matchless skill, of the Stranger of Galilee.

His look of compassion, His words of love, they shall not forgotten be, when sin-sick and helpless He saw me there, this Stranger of Galilee.

He showed me His hand and His riven side, and He whispered, 'It was for thee;' My burden fell off at the pierced feet, of the Stranger of Galilee.

And I felt I could love Him forever, so gracious and tender was He; I claimed Him that day as my Savior, this Stranger of Galilee."[182]

I replayed those words over and over in my mind. I asked myself the question, is it possible that *my* burden could fall off if I also saw the crucified Lamb at Calvary? The Tempter snuck up behind me and whispered in my left ear that The Prince would not do that for me. To my astonishment, at that very moment someone on my right gave me a note that had been passed down to me by a gentleman named Stuart Hamblen. I opened the message and excitedly read the following:

"*It is no secret what God can do.*"[183]

This penman pointed out that if The Conductor delivered other passengers, He could certainly provide that same salvation to me. I knew many viewed this "Stranger of Galilee" as someone easy to love. Before boarding this train, I had no issues with the Christ, but with those who carried His name and lived differently than He did. But on the *Ecclesia Express,* I had met so many who resembled their Master. When Mrs. Morris finished her speech, a gentleman whose name I did not catch spoke next. His talk was equally compelling:

"*I was a captive, but mercy released me, I was in darkness, but now I can see; Over the mountain where lonely I wandered, Jesus my Savior, came looking for me.*

Weeping, I longed for the rapture of pardon, longed from my burden of sin to be free; Then as I lifted my earnest petition, Jesus my Savior, came looking for me.

Filled with the fullness of perfect salvation, washed in the blood that was shed on the tree; This my rejoicing through ages eternal, Jesus my Savior, came looking for me."[184]

All along the journey I heard some passengers testify that "they found Him" while others asserted, "He found me." I tried to determine which sentiment was correct and had decided The Prince must have found the people, because we were the ones who were lost and not Him. However, I now realized that both descriptions remained aptly true. Although He was not lost, I was certainly searching for something, for *someone*, to satisfy the longings of my eternal soul. Wayward lives like mine searching for salvation made perfect sense. Yet what this speaker said seemed incomprehensible, that:

"Jesus my Savior, came looking for ME."

George Wright stepped forward as the third person to address our group. He picked right up where the previous speaker had finished and told us what The Prince did when He found us deeply lost in sin:

"Once my soul was astray from the heavenly way, I was wretched and vile as could be; but the Savior in love, gave me peace from above, When He reached down His hand for me.

When my Savior reached down for me, He had to reach way down for me; I was lost and undone, without God or His Son, When He reached down His hand for me."[185]

I thought again about the "Lost and Found" section of The Schedule and I pictured the shepherd reaching down to pick up the lost sheep and the woman reaching down to pick up her lost coin.[186] I had met a lot of people whose lives had been transformed by The Prince. He surely had to reach way down to lift them up, yet at that moment, I felt like I was in a deeper pit than anyone I had ever known. Could His blood really reach deeper than sin ever stained? Might His merciful arms be too short to reach me in my despair?

What happened next included a beautiful sequence of voices whispering gentle invitations for us to accept the offer of abundant life from The Prince of Calvary. The entire scene surely must have been orchestrated by My Companion, who was wooing me to surrender to the Savior. Rather than come up to the platform, these gentle voices were strategically placed throughout the Lounge and one-by-one, the inviters simply arose to their feet and extended to us an invitation to continue the trip to the Shining City. A man named Ralph Carmichael stood up, earnestly telling us:

"The Savior is waiting."[187]

He reminded the audience that The Prince has knocked at the doors of our hearts many times, seeking entrance into our lives.

Mary Slade immediately arose and echoed that same invitation:

"Who at my door is standing, patiently drawing near? Entrance within demanding, whose is the voice I hear?

Lonely without He's staying, lonely within am I; While I am still delaying, will He not pass me by?

Sweetly the tones are falling, open the door for Me; If thou wilt heed my calling, I will abide with Thee."[188]

The image of Christ knocking at the door of my heart easily came into my mind. I knew He had been patiently knocking and waiting on me for a long time. At that moment, Lelia Morris spoke up again. A few minutes ago, she told us about the "Stranger of Galilee." Once more she spoke with a heart-felt plea:

"If you are tired of the load of your sin, let Jesus come into your heart; If you desire a new life to begin, let Jesus come into your heart.

Just now, your doubtings give o'er, just now, reject Him no more; Just now, throw open the door, let Jesus come into your heart."[189]

How did she know I felt "tired of the load of my sin?" I must confess, I was oh so weary of juggling all the many bags of luggage I possessed. Could I truly ever be free from shame and guilt by simply opening a door? As this dear lady sat down, an older man named Joseph Hart began to speak. He was direct and to the point when he added:

"Come ye weary, heavy-laden, lost and ruined by the fall; If you tarry till you're better, you will never come at all."[190]

Again, it seemed as if every speaker was looking right into the depths of my soul. I had heard about people who felt they needed to improve on their own before coming to The Prince. Suddenly, I found myself having that same mindset. Despite what the Tempter kept saying to me, I knew Joseph Hart's words were true. While I contemplated such happenings, a familiar voice began to speak. It belonged to Aunt Fanny. Why should I have been surprised to see her present? She devoted much of her time to help with rescue operations for the lost. She, too, was invoking an invitation to us all. I never heard her speak with such tender compassion on our behalf:

> "*Pass me not, O gentle Savior, hear my humble cry; While on others Thou art calling, do not pass me by.*
>
> *Savior, Savior, hear my humble cry; While on others Thou art calling, do not pass me by.*"[191]

As she spoke, I recalled several people in The Schedule who called out to The Prince for help, and He always hearkened to their cry. I also remembered the writer saying that when The Prince walked on the water, He "would have passed them by" had they not cried out to Him.[192] Something inside of me wanted to cry out to Him too.

Two others stood up at the same time to issue forth their invitation. From the left side of the room, Will Thompson spoke first. I remembered him being at that initial breakfast I attended on the train. On that occasion he told us that Jesus was all the world to Him. He now painted an eloquent picture of The Prince wanting to save us too:

> "*Softly and tenderly Jesus is calling, calling for you and for me; See, on the portals He's waiting and watching, watching for you and for me.*
>
> *Come home, come home, you who are weary, come home; Earnestly, tenderly Jesus is calling, calling O sinner, come home.*"[193]

In answer to the Lord's call to come home, the man from the far right of the room gave the response. It was William J. Kirkpatrick who had begun the service by playing the piano. He replied:

"I've wandered far away from God, Lord, I'm coming home; The paths of sin too long I've trod, Lord, I'm coming home.

Coming home, coming home, never more to roam; Open wide Thine arms of love, Lord, I'm coming home."[194]

Again, his words sounded like what the prodigal was surely saying when he returned to his Father from the far country according to the Lost and Found section of The Schedule.[195]

A pause in the proceedings allowed me a few moments to look around and assess the situation. Some of those who had been summoned to hear the final invitations responded to them very quickly. I saw them signal a porter who stamped their ticket for "CALVARY" at the next stop. They seemed relieved and at ease with their choice. On the other hand, many who received the summons for this gathering did not even come to the meeting. They made their choice and their mouths filled with many excuses as to why they would not be getting off the train at the scene of the cross. Also, some who heard the exact same presentations that I did, decided the cost was too great to continue the journey. One by one, these men and women got up and walked to a different part of the train.[196] I suddenly noticed Mr. P.P. Bliss take the microphone on the platform. On my first evening aboard the *Ecclesia Express,* he had told me about the glories of The Conductor and His beloved Son, The Prince. His repeated words "Hallelujah, what a Savior" echoed many times in my mind. He proved a fitting choice to make a final appeal to us:

"Free from the law, O happy condition, Jesus has bled and there is remission; Cursed by the law and bruised by the fall, Grace has redeemed us once for all.

"Once for all, O sinner, receive it; Once for all, O friend, now believe it; Cling to the cross, the burden will fall, Christ has redeemed us once for all."[197]

Again, I heard that promise: "the burden will fall." Mr. Bliss shared the Good News in the most wonderful of ways. But just then, he sounded a minor chord as he reminded us of the fate awaiting those who make the wrong decision concerning whether to stop at Calvary:

> "*Almost persuaded now to believe; Almost persuaded, Christ to receive; Seems now some soul to say, 'Go, Spirit, go Thy way, Some more convenient day, on Thee I'll call.'*
>
> *Almost persuaded, harvest is past; Almost persuaded, doom comes at last; Almost cannot avail, Almost is but to fail, Sad, sad, that bitter wail, Almost but lost.*"[198]

Like the heathen king who answered the apostle thusly long ago, so also many of us in that room sat in the valley of decision.[199] Some of us lived not far from the kingdom.[200] Calvary awaited just one stop ahead! On the other hand, to be "almost persuaded" is to be altogether lost. It was not just the sweetly worded invitations that we needed to hear. We also needed to be reminded of the consequences of making no decision, which in fact is the wrong decision. A Mr. Shadduck followed Mr. Bliss's somber words with an even more frightening forecast:

> "*I dreamed of the great judgment morning, had dawned and the trumpet had blown, I dreamed that the nations had gathered, to judgment before the white throne.*
>
> *From the throne came a bright, shining angel, and he stood on the land and the sea; And he swore with his hand raised to Heaven, that time was no longer to be.*
>
> *And oh, what a weeping and wailing, as the lost were told of their fate; They cried for the rocks and the mountains, they prayed, but their prayer was too late.*"[201]

His words shook me deeply, as I was overwhelmed with the thought of one day standing before The Great Conductor and giving an account of my life to Him. I remembered later that the half-brother of The Prince once wrote that some could be saved by responding to compassion, while others would have to be saved by fear, as being pulled right out of the fire.[202] This seemed to be happening at this moment. My Companion explored every possible way to reach my heart and I felt tugged back and forth. At that moment, the train sounded a loud whistle and one of the porters came into the Lounge Car and shouted that the next stop would be Calvary and that all passengers getting off there would need to have their ticket stamped accordingly. My Companion, who had encouraged me to board the train in the first place continued to urge me to go to the cross. The Tempter also remained present, trying to get me to focus on all the passengers who had decided to avoid that stop, even if it meant their life would be spent going in the opposite direction of the Shining City. The porters remained helpful, always pointing to the life changing truths found in The Schedule. All this special session in the Lounge Car greatly impacted me. However, the closing words from four different ladies ultimately "sealed the deal" for me and prompted me to make a defining decision. First, came Elizabeth Reed. I am not even sure she planned to speak. She stood up and with tears in her eyes pleaded with those of us who remained seated:

> *"Oh, do not let the word depart, and close thine eyes against the light; Poor sinner, harden not your heart, Be saved, O tonight.*
>
> *Oh, why not tonight? Oh, why not tonight? Wilt thou be saved? Then why not tonight?*
>
> *"Tomorrow's sun may never rise, to bless thy long-deluded sight; This is the time, O then be wise, Be saved, O tonight."*[203]

Her eyes were not the only ones swelling up with tears. "Tomorrow's sun may never rise" gripped my spirit. No passenger on the train, be they saint or sinner, has the promise of tomorrow. No wonder The Schedule clearly identified today as the "day of salvation."[204] As I thought about her question, I could come up with no answer for Elizabeth Reed. The second woman, whose words pushed me toward a decision, spoke next. Charlotte

Elliott sat in a wheelchair in the Lounge Car. I understood that she spent
most of her trip on the train confined to her berth in the Sleeping Car.
Although an invalid, stricken with an extensive illness, she not only told us
why we should come to Calvary, she told us how to do it:

> *"Just as I am without one plea, but that Thy blood was shed for me;
> And that Thou bidst me come to Thee, O Lamb of God, I come, I come.*
>
> *Just as I am and waiting not, to rid my soul of one dark blot; To Thee
> whose blood can cleanse each spot, O Lamb of God, I come, I come.*
>
> *Just as I am though tossed about, with many a conflict, many a doubt;
> Fightings and fears within, without, O Lamb of God, I come, I come.*
>
> *Just as I am Thou wilt receive, Wilt welcome pardon, cleanse, relieve;
> Because Thy promise I believe, O Lamb of God, I come, I come."*[205]

By this time, my heart turned toward Home! I knew I needed to
come to the Lamb. My baggage that I believed to be so valuable became
worthless junk that I needed to surrender to Him.[206] Just when I did not
think I could take any more without yielding in complete submission to
The Prince, another woman named Elizabeth announced that she wanted
to tell us a story:

> *"There were ninety and nine that safely lay in the shelter of the fold, but
> one was out on the hills away, far off from the gates of gold.*
>
> *Away on the mountains wild and bare, away from the tender
> Shepherd's care.*
>
> *Lord, Thou hast here Thy ninety and nine, are they not enough for
> Thee, But the shepherd made answer 'This of mine has wandered away
> from Me.'*
>
> *And although the road be rough and steep, I go to the desert to find
> My sheep.*

But none of the ransomed ever knew how deep were the waters crossed, Nor how dark was the night that the Lord passed through, ere He found His sheep that was lost.

Far out in the desert He heard its cry, 'Twas sick and helpless and ready to die.

Lord, whence are those blood-drops all the way, that mark out the mountain's track? They were shed for one who had gone astray, ere the Shepherd could bring him back.

Lord, whence are Thy hands so rent and torn? They're pierced tonight by many a thorn.

And all through the mountains thunder riven and up from the rocky steep, There arose a glad cry to the gate of Heaven, 'Rejoice! I have found My sheep!'

And the angels echoed around the throne, 'Rejoice, for the Lord brings back His own.'"[207]

I had read that story many times in the Lost and Found section of The Schedule.[208] I had heard the porters talk about it to others. But I had never heard it told like this second Elizabeth had just shared with us. This time it was not about someone else, on the contrary, this time the name of the lost sheep was ME. The Prince not only came looking for me, He left 99 others to do so. I began to think about the 99. I thought of all the prophets, priests, kings, apostles, evangelists, pastors, and teachers listed in The Schedule and how He left them all for me. My mind raced from person to person that I had met on this train since I first boarded it long ago. I thought of Aunt Fanny, Charles Wesley, Mr. Bliss, Isaac Watts, Preacher Chapman, Longfellow, Newton, Reverend Lowry, Young Bill, and many more – The Shepherd-Prince left them all to look for me! What was it Elizabeth just said? "None of the ransomed ever knew how deep were the waters or how dark was the night" that the Shepherd went through for me. Only Jesus, The Crown Prince could possibly know how costly the price that He paid to redeem His lost sheep.[209] I knew I must go to Calvary to thank Him and pledge my life to Him forever.

While trembling with a fountain of tears, I summoned a porter to go and retrieve my excess baggage. He stamped my ticket for Calvary and proceeded to go and get my huge amount of luggage that covered my berth in the Sleeping Car. At that precise moment, I heard the train come to a screeching halt. There were only a handful of people still left in the Lounge Car. Some of them embraced me with joy because of my decision. I saw the Tempter slink away from the room in defeat and disgust. My Companion re-appeared and seemed happier than I had ever seen him. As we arose and prepared to leave the Lounge Car, the fourth woman spoke the final word. What Mrs. Rhea Miller said became the words my heart was extolling as I headed for the cross.

> "I'd rather have Jesus than silver or gold, I'd rather be His than have riches untold; I'd rather have Jesus than houses or lands, I'd rather be led by His nail-pierced hand.
>
> I'd rather have Jesus than men's applause, I'd rather be faithful to His dear cause; I'd rather have Jesus than world-wide fame, I'd rather be true to His holy name.
>
> Than to be the king of a vast domain or be held in sin's dread sway; I'd rather have Jesus than anything the world affords today."[210]

Just then the porter came in, pushing a huge cart filled with my excessive belongings. I glanced at them one last time and then I looked around at the passengers who loved The Prince. Just as Moses and many others made this same choice, I knew that I had made the right decision.[211] I clutched The Schedule to my heart, wiped the tears from my eyes, whispered the name of My Prince, and started toward the exit door to a place called Calvary.

Chapter Nine –

CALVARY

I could not begin to tell you how much my life changed by that one stop at Calvary. I left the train burdened with heavy baggage. When I returned, I felt light and free. Many of us came back together, each rejoicing at what had happened to us all. To our surprise, many passengers gathered outside the train entrance to welcome us back and to escort us to a special reception prepared in the Lounge Car. As we neared the door, cheers and applause began to burst forth from the crowd that greeted us with warm smiles and much fanfare. The praises came not for us, but for The Prince, who had "done it again" in providing forgiveness and redemption to wayward souls. A stranger in the midst who did not know what transpired cried out to us, "Where have you all been?" Young Bill was the first to answer for us:

"I've been to Calvary."[212]

He then shared some of what happened to him when he previously stopped at the cross.

We all nodded our heads in agreement, but the questioner appeared puzzled by his response. James Rowe was standing nearby. He explained that we, who were returning from this train stop, could now assert:

"I'm redeemed by love divine, glory, glory, Christ is mine; All to Him I now resign, I have been redeemed."[213]

When each one of us went through the door of the train we met with someone to personally escort us to the testimony reception in the Lounge Car. Some of the newborn believers could not wait until they arrived at the venue, they lifted their voices while we proceeded to the gala. I heard Rufus McDaniel from near the front of the line. He shouted to all who could hear him:

"What a wonderful change in my life has been wrought, since Jesus came into my heart; I have light in my soul for which long I have sought, since Jesus came into my heart.

I have ceased from my wandering and going astray, since Jesus came into my heart; And my sins which were many are all washed away, since Jesus came into my heart.

I shall go there to dwell in that City I know, since Jesus came into my heart; And I'm happy, so happy as onward I go, since Jesus came into my heart."[214]

I stood amazed to hear others express exactly what happened to me. A Mr. Vandall was walking close by. (I found out later his real name was Napoleon Bonaparte, however, he went by N.B. – his initials only.) He not only rejoiced because The Prince came into his heart, he expressed delight because something had been removed:

"My sins are gone."[215]

The new convert took joy in knowing his transgressions were vanquished, never to be remembered by the Conductor again.

What a wondrous thought! One moment ten thousand sins stood against my name and the next moment none condemned me! I always heard that the secret of traveling right is to travel light. I no longer carried guilt and shame and disgrace and a dozen other unsightly bags. Now I could go to see The Prince who separated me from all those struggles. When we finally reached the Lounge Car, the room filled up with even more well-wishers. This was a party like no other in my lifetime! One of the porters read from the "Lost and Found" section of The Schedule.[216] Another told the attendees that news about what happened again at Calvary already reached the Shining City. He informed the celebrants that the inhabitants of our destination even now rejoiced over our salvation.[217] After another spontaneous shout of victory, they escorted us up on to a stage to sit before the people. The porter asked if any of us wanted to tell what had happened to us on that hill of redemption. C. Austin Miles jumped up from the crowd and wanted to go first. He was the man who shared with me about the resurrection garden on the first Lord's Day. Even though he had been to Calvary long ago, he testified as if he just arrived back from there the first time:

> "I was once a sinner, but I came, pardon to receive from my Lord; This was freely given, and I found, that He always kept His Word… In the Book 'tis written, 'Saved by grace,' O the joy that came to my soul; Now I am forgiven, and I know, by the blood I am made whole.
>
> There's a new name written down in glory, and it's mine, O yes, it's mine, And the white-robed angels sing the story, a sinner has come home; For there's a new name written down in glory, and it's mine, O yes it's mine; With my sins forgiven, I am bound for Heaven, nevermore to roam."[218]

Before Brother Miles could sit down, Elisha Hoffman stood up and cried:

"It is mine, mine, blessed be His name, He has given peace, perfect peace to me; It is mine, mine, blessed be His name, mine for all eternity.

"God's abiding peace is in my soul today, yes, I feel it now, yes, I feel it now; He has taken all my doubts and fears away, though I cannot tell you how."[219]

Some of the testimonies focused on what The Prince removed from us, and others pointed to what He bestowed to us. Before going to Calvary, we were not only depraved, but deprived. We not only needed something taken out; we needed something put in. And The Prince did that very thing for us! A fellow named James Sullivan was sitting next to me. When it came his turn, he said:

"There is a song in my heart today, something I never had; Jesus has taken my sins away, O say but I'm glad... O say but I'm glad, I'm glad, O say but I'm glad.

Jesus has come and my cup's overrun, O say but I'm glad."[220]

Everyone appeared overcome with great joy. I also marveled that those hearing the testimonies seemed as excited as those sharing them. They never seemed to get tired of hearing the similar accounts of transformation. Charles Gabriel had long ago stopped at Calvary. He spoke at the table during my first breakfast on the train. On that occasion he expressed amazement at being in the presence of Jesus the Nazarene. He lived as a faithful follower of The Prince. Yet he could not contain himself to merely listen, so he called out from the audience:

"In loving kindness Jesus came, my soul in mercy to reclaim; And from the depths of sin and shame, through grace He lifted me.

From sinking sand He lifted me, with tender hand He lifted me; From shades of night to plains of light, O praise His name, He lifted me."[221]

It was not only men who made the trek to the cross. A woman named Clara Williams testified about her encounter with The Prince:

"Hallelujah! I have found Him, Whom my soul so long has craved; Jesus satisfies my longings, through His blood I now am saved."[222]

Another brother named Jack echoed that same sentiment:

"I've found a Friend, who is all to me, His love is ever true; I love to tell how He lifted me and what His grace can do for you.

Saved by His power divine, saved to new life sublime; Life now is sweet, and my joy is complete, for I'm saved, saved, saved."[223]

I knew many different theological terms and metaphors used to describe the wondrous experience that initiates a person into the family of The Conductor and His Son, The Prince. The one that seemingly arose above the others was the language of salvation or of "being saved."[224] Elisha Hoffman leaped back up a second time and declared:

"Down at the cross where my Savior died, down where for cleansing from sin I cried; There to my heart was the blood applied, glory to His Name.

I am so wondrously saved from sin, Jesus so sweetly abides within; There at the cross where He took me in, glory to His Name..."[225]

Brother Hoffman then pointed to the assembly and, perchance someone else needed to go to the cross, he added:

"Come to this fountain so rich and sweet, cast thy poor soul at the Savior's feet; Plunge in today and be made complete, glory to His Name."[226]

I had not seen Philip Doddridge since the earlier chapel on Grace. He chimed in with what happened to him also:

"O happy day, that fixed my choice, on Thee, my Savior, and my God; Happy day, happy day, When Jesus washed my sins away.

It's done, the great transaction's done, I am the Lord's, and He is mine;
He drew me, and I followed on, charmed to confess the voice divine."[227]

I said "amen" to all of these assertions, especially Doddridge's observation that the "great transaction" is an accomplished fact. The fish is in the water and the water is in the fish. The bird is in the air and the air is in the bird. The plant is in the soil and the soil is in the plant. I am now in the Lord, and He is in me! Lelia Morris added her insights in the middle of the celebration. She was one of those present in that same Lounge Car earlier urging us to stop at Calvary. On this occasion she shouted out:

"Bethlehem, Calvary, Olivet, tell, O what a Savior is mine; Mountain
and plain with His praises shall swell, O what a Savior is mine.

There on the cross where He died for my sin, O what a Savior is mine;
Giving His life a poor wanderer to win, O what a Savior is mine."[228]

She was right. The cross forever verifies the greatness of our Savior-Prince. I too shared my testimony. I spoke from the heart, but my remarks lacked both the eloquence and theological depth of most of the other speakers. Yet we were not competing against each other. Every soul mattered to The Prince – including mine! A younger man, John Peterson, was the last person to testify at the party. After hearing his words, I felt they saved the best for last when he said:

"Heaven came down and glory filled my soul."[229]

This eloquent expression seemed to summarize in a single sentence what happened to me that day.

Again, people kept speaking about the transaction. Because of His grace, we easily realized the best end of the exchange. The Prince took our sins, and we received His salvation. Praises continued to rise to our triumphant Victor as the gathering came to an end. After some of us believed on the Lamb at Calvary, we were baptized by one of the porters before we re-boarded the train. For those not yet baptized, they were invited to proceed to a special car where a porter waited to baptize them before the train left the station again. As that small group made their way with a guide, named Ernest Blandy, I heard him leading that collection of candidates in, saying:

> *"I can hear my Savior calling, I can hear my Savior calling; I can hear my Savior calling, Take my cross and follow, follow Me.*
>
> *Where He leads me I will follow, where He leads me I will follow; Where He leads me I will follow, I'll go with Him, with Him, all the way."*[230]

As for me, I felt wide awake and greatly invigorated. I headed for the Communication Car to spend a little more time in worship and adoration to the One who brought me so far and changed my life forever. Margaret Harris went to the cross with us. She only testified briefly at the reception but must have had the same idea that I did. As she walked about ten yards ahead of me toward the place of worship, she evidently could not wait to lift her voice in gratitude to her Redeemer. During the party she said:

> *"When I saw the cleansing fountain, open wide for all my sin; I obeyed the Spirit's wooing, when He said, 'Will thou be clean?'"*[231]

Now, she opened her voice to express her response to what The Prince had granted her:

> *"I will praise Him, I will praise Him, Praise the Lamb for sinners slain; Give Him glory all ye people, for His blood can wash away each stain."*[232]

I, too, found myself freely magnifying the Savior even before entering The Conductor's Car. After an extended time of conversation with the King, I went to my room to retire for the night. It surely ranked as the most wonderful of all days and I did not want it to end. However, I knew a lifetime of blessed days awaited as I now had a new purpose and destiny. As I prepared to lay down and sleep, I remembered what someone at the party had said:

"Now I belong to Jesus."[233]

For the first in my life, I put my head on the pillow at night knowing that for certain. And equally amazing, The Prince belonged to me. That served as a perfect message for me to meditate on until sleep came to me as a most welcome guest.

Chapter Ten –

DISCIPLESHIP

Everything seemed new and wonderful and different after my stop at Calvary. I understood why The Schedule called this conversion experience a "new birth."[234] I began to grow in my relationship with The Prince. I looked forward to frequent times of conversation as I spoke to Him (via prayer in The Communication Car) and He spoke to me (through reading even the "fine print" of The Schedule). Instead of only visiting the chapel services periodically, I anticipated being present for each of them. One of the events that caused me to grow in my faith the most occurred at the Table of Remembrance. At regular times, believing passengers would assemble in the Chapel Car to sit with one another and recall the incalculable price The Prince paid in providing for their redemption.

I witnessed a couple of these episodes before, but always from a distance. Now, for the first time I felt somewhat comfortable in occupying a place at the Table. My first communion aboard the *Ecclesia Express* became memorable. I took my seat at the Table just before the sacred service began. Someone I did not know opened the event in prayer:

"We gather together to ask the Lord's blessing, He chastens and hastens His will to make known; The wicked oppressing now cease from distressing, sing praises to His name, He forgets not His own.

Beside us to guide us, our God with us joining, ordaining, maintaining His kingdom divine; So from the beginning the fight we were winning, Thou, Lord, were at our side, all glory be Thine."[235]

A couple of porters distributed the elements of the unleavened bread and the pure fruit juices of the vine. One of them read from one of the Good News accounts in The Schedule and another from one of the ancient apostle's letters to a long-ago passenger train.[236] As we consumed the elements accordingly, M.S. Lemons shared all our sentiments in a somber tone:

"I remember how my Savior died for me, on the rugged cross of dark Mount Calvary; I remember how He cried, how He bowed His head and died, I remember dark Calvary.

I remember how He paid the debt for me, how His blood was shared on dark Calvary; O the blood of Calvary's brow, I can see it flowing now, I remember dark Calvary.

I remember how He blessed and broke the bread, signifies my broken body, thus He said; Broken on the cruel tree, hanging there for you and me, I remember dark Calvary.

I remember how He blessed the cup of wine, that which is the precious fruitage of the vine; O this is my blood, He said, and for many it was shed, I remember dark Calvary."[237]

Both of my eyes flooded with tears as I rehearsed in my mind what I witnessed when I climbed the hill at Calvary. Elvina Hall sat across from me. She burst out with a loud voice:

"Jesus paid it all, All to Him I owe; Sin had left a crimson stain, He washed it white as snow.

For nothing good have I, whereby Thy grace to claim; I'll wash my garments white, in the blood of Calvary's Lamb.

And when before the throne, I stand in Him complete; 'Jesus died my soul to save,' my lips shall still repeat.

Jesus paid it all, All to Him I owe; Sin had left a crimson stain, He washed it white as snow."[238]

Several others seated near me also testified about what The Prince had done for them. Adger Pace said:

"He's my King,"[239]

"Jesus is the One,"[240] and *"Victory Today is Mine."*[241]

He reflected on his own conversion by saying:

"I can tell you the time."[242]

He then proceeded to tell us about the moment he met The Prince.

Frank Graham offered a similar personal story:

"Long ago, long ago, yes the old account was settled long ago; And the record's clear today, for He washed my sins away, When the old account was settled long ago."[243]

A delightful old gentleman named G.T. Speer shared similar sentiments. (Many people called him "Dad Speer" because his family and children were well known believers.) He referred to The Prince as,

"The Dearest Friend I Ever Had."[244]

Like the others before him, Dad Speer said:

"I Never Shall Forget the Day."[245]

The day that he referenced pointed to when the burden of his sins rolled away. All of us around the table could recall that marvelous hour.

For the next several minutes, I could no longer hear what else was being said. My mind traveled back to what my life was like before I met The Prince. I thought of those heavy bags of sins and weights that I carried around for so long and how they all dropped off me when I gazed at the Lord dying on the tree for me. The memory of that moment remains forever fixed in my heart. When my attention came back to my surroundings at the Table, I heard Minnie Steele's voice coming from one end of the room. I thought she must be reading my mind when she said:

"*I remember when my burdens rolled away, I had carried them for years night and day; When I sought the blessed Lord, and I took Him at His word, then at once all my burdens rolled away.*

I remember when my burdens rolled away, that I feared would never leave, night or day; Jesus showed to me the loss, so I left them at the cross, I was glad when my burdens rolled away.

I remember when my burdens rolled away, that had hindered me for years night and day; As I sought the throne of grace, just a glimpse of Jesus' face, And I knew that my burdens could not stay.

I am singing since my burdens rolled away, there's a song within my heart night and day; I am living for my King, and with joy I shout and sing, 'Hallelujah, all my burdens rolled away.'"[246]

I realized that every time I could join my brothers and sisters at the Table, it would be like going back to Calvary all over again. Another woman, Jennie Hussey, followed Minnie and said:

"*King of my life, I crown Thee now, Thine shall the glory be; Lest I forget Thy thorn-crowned brow, Lead me to Calvary.*

Lest I forget Gethsemane, lest I forget Thine agony; Lest I forget Thy love for me, Lead me to Calvary."[247]

How could anyone ever forget how The Prince prayed in the garden and how He suffered on the tree? Calvary could never be a place where someone could visit and then blot out the trip from their memory. After the two women had spoken, a porter asked Aunt Fanny to share a word. She sat at the far end of the Table, and I had not noticed her presence. She added this prayer and admonition:

> *"Jesus, keep me near the cross, there a precious fountain; Free to all, a healing stream, flows from Calvary's mountain.*
>
> *In the cross, in the cross, be my glory ever; Till my raptured soul shall find rest beyond the river.*
>
> *Near the cross, O Lamb of God, bring its scenes before me; Help me walk from day to day, with its shadows o'er me.*
>
> *Near the cross I'll watch and wait, hoping, trusting ever; Till I reach the golden strand, just beyond the river."*[248]

Aunt Fanny always seemed to have just the right words to say. Her speech concluded with a reference to the Shining City, which was a fitting tie-in how the Table of Remembrance event ended. The presiding porter pointed us back to the fine print in The Schedule that said we were to keep meeting at the Table to remember –

"Until He comes."[249]

A Brother Winsett stood to remind us of that:

> *"We're looking for His coming in the clouds of Heaven, coming back to earth to catch away His own; Then may we all be ready when the midnight cry is given, to go and reign with Christ on His throne.*
>
> *Gladly may we herald the message of His blessed appearing, soon He's coming in glory, tell to one and all; Then awake ye saints of the Lord, why stumble when the end is nearing, But get ready for the final call."*[250]

Thus, I learned at my first communion experience that each time may be the last one. One of the porters asked a brother named Vaughan to give the benediction. Part of his closing remarks included:

"There's a blessed time that's coming, coming soon, it may be evening, morning, or at noon; The wedding of the bride, united with the Groom, we shall see the King when He comes.

We shall see the King, we shall see the King, we shall see the King when He comes; He is coming in power, we'll hail the blessed hour, We shall see the King when He comes."[251]

The Table of Remembrance became one of my most cherished times and places along the journey. It proved to be a blessed occasion to reflect on the past (The Prince on the Tree), the present (The Prince at the Table), and the future (The Prince on the Throne).

As a new member in the family of The Conductor, I needed much help to grow and mature in the abundant life I now lived. The train carried a great number of passengers who modeled the Christian life for me. Also, like most new converts, I needed a mentor to guide me in the early days of my adventure in the faith. I found such a person in a man named Johnson Oatman. He previously became ordained as a minister but had never served as a porter on a train. Rather, Brother Oatman became a successful businessman who knew The Schedule well and could communicate it clearly to inform and inspire others. I am not sure how we exactly met, but I do remember when he offered to meet with me individually to encourage me in my new lifestyle. Since I had heard of so many people on the train who had been discipled by a consecrated believer, I eagerly accepted his offer and looked forward to our visits. We shared three special appointments in a one-on-one setting.

Our first meeting together took place in the Coach Car. We sat across from one another as the train traveled through a picturesque part of the country. Brother Oatman (all the "misters" in the family became "brothers" after Calvary) emphasized the importance of my relationship with The Prince. He described it as a special friendship. He showed me from the old section of The Schedule that "there is a friend that sticks closer than a brother."[252] He then showed me from the Good News that The Prince

Himself has called us His friends.[253] He convinced me that the Lord allows us to get as close to Him as we choose to do so:

> "*They tried my Lord and Master, with no one to defend; Within the halls of Pilate, He stood without a friend.*
>
> *The world may turn against Him, I'll love Him to the end; And while on earth I'm living, my Lord shall have a friend.*
>
> *I'll do what He may bid me, I'll go where He may send; I'll try each flying moment, to prove that I'm His friend.*
>
> *To all who need a Savior, my Friend I'll recommend; Because He brought salvation, is why I am His friend.*
>
> *I'll be a friend to Jesus, my life for Him I'll spend; I'll be a friend to Jesus, until my days shall end.*"[254]

Brother Oatman assigned me a reading from The Schedule. He then gave me a test with ten questions about The Prince. The answer to every question was "*No, not One.*"

> "*There's not a friend like the lowly Jesus. None else could heal all our soul's diseases. (No, not One)*
>
> *No friend like Him is so high and holy. And yet no friend is so meek and lowly. (No, not One)*
>
> *There's not an hour that He is not near us. No night so dark but His love can cheer us. (No, not One)*
>
> *Did ever saint find this Friend forsake him? Or sinner find that He would not take him? (No, not One)*
>
> *Was e'er a gift like the Savior given? Will He refuse us a home in Heaven? (No, not One)*"[255]

I felt pleased that I answered every question correctly. I learned this first lesson well: Jesus is the closest friend anyone could ever have.

After over an hour of inspirational dialogue, we prayed together and each of us went our separate ways. Our next meeting was held about a week later. We agreed to meet in the Dining Car for breakfast together. In this second session, Johnson Oatman stressed to me the importance of prayer and praise to The Conductor, as well as the need to maintain an exemplary attitude around fellow passengers on the train. He made it clear that despite life's difficulties, our blessings far outnumber our trials. He gave me this challenge:

> "When upon life's billows you are tempest-tossed, when you are discouraged, thinking all is lost; Count your many blessings, name them one by one, and it will surprise you what the Lord has done.
>
> Count your blessings, name them one by one, count your blessings, see what God has done.
>
> Count your blessings, name them one by one, count your many blessings, see what God has done."[256]

He then admonished me never to envy the treasures that others seemingly hold. Rather, we are to remember just how blessed we who know The Prince truly are:

> "When you look at others with their lands and gold, think that Christ has promised you His wealth untold; Count your many blessings money cannot buy, your reward in Heaven, nor your home on high."[257]

Brother Oatman then shared his personal testimony with me:

> "Once a sinner far from Jesus I was perishing with cold, but the blessed Savior heard me when I cried.
>
> Then He threw His robe around me, and He led me to His fold, and I'm living on the Hallelujah Side.
>
> Oh, glory be to Jesus, let the hallelujahs roll, help me ring the Savior's praises far and wide.

For I've opened up toward Heaven all the windows of my soul, and I'm living on the Hallelujah Side."[258]

The Hallelujah Side! Leave it to my friend and mentor to come up with a name for his new address since being rescued by The Prince. He added these insights as well:

"Not for all earth's golden millions would I leave this precious place, though the tempter to persuade me oft has tried.

For I'm safe in God's pavilion, happy in His love and grace, and I'm living on the Hallelujah Side.

Here the sun is always shining, here the sky is always bright, 'Tis no place for gloomy Christians to abide.

For my soul is filled with music and my heart with great delight, And I'm living on the Hallelujah Side."[259]

The thought of a "gloomy Christian" seemed impossible to me – especially aboard the *Ecclesia Express*. I soon learned what he said about The Tempter was also true. He did not leave me alone after I surrendered to The Prince. In fact, he bothered me more than ever after my stop at Calvary. Once again, I gained so much from these one-on-one sessions together.

Our last meeting took place a few days later in the Lounge Car. It usually is somewhat loud in that room, but we chose a time when the crowds had not yet gathered. During this visit, my mentor admonished me never to become content spiritually, but rather to always forge ahead. He explained his reasoning this way:

"I'm pressing on the upward way, new heights I'm gaining every day; Still praying as I onward bound, 'Lord, plant my feet on higher ground.'

Lord, lift me up and let me stand, by faith on Heaven's table land; A higher plane than I have found, Lord, plant my feet on higher ground.

My heart has no desire to stay, where doubts arise and fears dismay; Though some may dwell where these abound, my prayer, my aim, is higher ground.

I want to live above the world, though Satan's darts at me are hurled; For faith has caught the joyful sound, the song of saints on higher ground.

I want to scale the utmost height and catch a gleam of glory bright; But still I'll pray till Heaven I've found, 'Lord, lead me on to higher ground.'"[260]

Of all the things he taught me, that remained with me the most... unless it was his exhortation for me to always keep the Shining City in view as my real home:

"I am thinking of the rapture in our blessed home on high, when the redeemed are gathering in; How we'll raise the heavenly anthem in that city in the sky,

When the redeemed are gathering in...

There will be a great procession over on the streets of gold, when the redeemed are gathering in; Oh, what music, Oh, what singing, o'er the city will be rolled,

When the redeemed are gathering in...

Saints will sing redemption's story with their voices clear and strong, when the redeemed are gathering in; Then the angels all will listen for they cannot join that song,

When the redeemed are gathering in...

Then the Savior will give orders to prepare the banquet board, when the redeemed are gathering in; And we'll hear His invitation, 'Come ye blessed of the Lord,'

When the redeemed are gathering in."[261]

My mentor made the Shining City seem so real. He shared one final personal message with me to end our scheduled sessions:

"Every cross that I bear for my Savior, will at last when He calls be laid down; And my sorrows will all be forgotten, when I trade the old cross for a crown."[262]

All my luggage that I left at Calvary pales in comparison to the glories waiting for us in the Shining City. I hated to see our discipleship times come to an end. How grateful I felt for the privilege to sit and learn from someone so strong in the faith. My Companion whispered to me that the time would come soon when the roles would reverse, and I could have the honor of mentoring some soul new in the faith.

Chapter Eleven –
HOLINESS

Every day of my new life provided the possibility of a new adventure. One such day stood out among the others. Early in the morning I arose to spend some time in the Communication Car conversing with The Conductor. While there, I noticed again the giant banner hanging on the wall above the prominent screens. I always read the large words on the impressive scroll, but this time I caught a glimpse of the smaller print below:

"Take time to be holy, speak oft with thy Lord, abide in Him always, and feed on His Word.

Make friends of God's children, help those who are weak, forgetting in nothing His blessing to seek."[263]

I asked one of the porters about the source of the sayings. He identified a former passenger by the name of William Longstaff as the penman. The porter then said, "Wait here, please" and left for a short time before returning with a card for me. He explained that Brother Longstaff wrote additional wording too vast to find inclusion on the banner. When I opened the card, I felt equally challenged to read his remarks, including:

"Take time to be holy, the world rushes on, spend much time in secret, with Jesus alone. By looking to Jesus, like Him thou shalt be, thy friends in thy conduct His likeness shall see."[264]

When I read that last line, I cried out,

"That is it. That is what I want the most – others to see The Prince when they look at me."

Later that morning I attended the Lord's Day Chapel. The announced theme consisted of one word: "Holiness." The only seat available happened to be near the front, right in the middle of a group of teen-aged young people. I gladly took the last available chair. One of the porters opened the session by reading many prominent passages about the topic from The Schedule.[265] To my delight, Mrs. Lelia Morris arose to speak after the sharing of the Scriptures. She eloquently told us about "The Stranger of Galilee" and then challenged us to "Let Jesus into our hearts" on that occasion when I punched my ticket for Calvary. I could never forget the details of that day! In this moment, she again had something worthwhile to say:

> *"'Called unto holiness' church of our God, Purchase of Jesus, redeemed by His blood; Called from the world and its idols to flee, Called from the bondage of sin to be free.*
>
> *'Holiness unto the Lord' is our watchword and song, 'Holiness unto the Lord' as we're marching along; Sing it, shout it, loud and long, 'Holiness unto the Lord' now and forever.*
>
> *'Called unto holiness,' bride of the Lamb, Waiting the Bridegroom's returning again, Lift up your heads for the day draweth near, When in His beauty the King shall appear."*[266]

As I listened to her stirring rendition, the difference between singing about holiness and living it came to my mind. The former appears easier, while the latter proves more difficult. Sister Morris finished her presentation with a flourish.

Suddenly, as if on cue, the group of young people surrounding me stood up and began to march down the aisle and across the stage. As they did, they chanted in unison:

"It's a highway to Heaven."[267]

They proclaimed only the pure in heart could be found walking on the King's Highway.

This kind of outburst usually did not happen in the chapel service. However, on this occasion it met with smiles and agreement from most of the attendees. We all knew we were on the King's railway to the Shining City and His people behaved holy.

After the young group returned to their seats, the porter introduced the main speaker for the session, a brother named Cyrus Nusbaum. He too spoke of the necessity of a holy life. He emphasized that obedience to the Master is the key to such victorious living. He challenged us with nine frequently asked questions – then provided the answer to all of them.

> *"Would you live for Jesus and be always pure and good? Would you walk with Him within the narrow road? Would you have Him bear your burden, carry all your load?*
>
> *Let Him have His way with thee.*
>
> *Would you have Him make you free and follow at His call? Would you know the peace that comes by giving all? Would you have Him save you so that you need never fall?*
>
> *Let Him have His way with thee.*
>
> *Would you in His kingdom find a place of constant rest? Would you prove Him true in providential test? Would you in His service always labor at your best?*
>
> *Let Him have His way with thee.*

His power can make you what you ought to be, His blood can cleanse your heart and make you free; His love can fill your soul and you will see,

'Twas best for Him to have His way with thee."[267]

A woman they called Adelaide Pollard closed the session with a responsive benediction. She prayed:

"Have Thine own way, Lord, have Thine own way, Thou art the Potter, I am the clay; Mold me and make me, after Thy will, While I am waiting, yielded and still."[268]

As we all turned to leave the Chapel Car upon dismissal, a gentleman named Howard Grose came up to the teen-agers and challenged them to:

"Give of your best to the Master, give of the strength of your youth; Clad in salvation's full armor, join in the battle for truth."[270]

I knew he intended his admonition for the young people, yet because I considered myself somewhat new in the faith, I personalized it as well.

Later that day, I passed by Mr. Albert E. Brumley sitting in his usual spot in the corner. I stopped and spoke with him for a few minutes. At one point I asked him if he had any regrets being on this train. Without hesitation he replied:

"I've never been sorry."[271]

I marveled at his declaration. He continued to speak glowingly about living for The Prince.

He added: *"It's a grand and glorious feeling"*[272] to belong to the Conductor.

My time on the *Ecclesia Express* could not compare with his in length, however, I shared his assessment about serving The Prince. Evidently young Bill possessed a similar view. I ran into him a few minutes later and he said the same thing to me in a slightly different way:

"The longer I serve Him the sweeter He grows."[273]

I heard of some who had stopped at Calvary who later returned to their previous ways.[274] Thankfully, I no longer desired all that baggage that used to fill up my life. However, I still struggled with some of my attitudes, actions, and reactions toward others. Specifically, I knew I needed to forgive some people. However, I always found a way to justify not doing it. At the same time, My Companion constantly tugged at my heart each time I stumbled, slipped, or fell. He gently reminded me that I now belonged to The Prince and my conduct should mirror that of the citizens of the Shining City. Even though I already spent part of the morning in the Communication Car in prayer to The Conductor, I felt led to go there again in the afternoon.

Just before I arrived at the prayer car, I came upon Aunt Fanny, sitting with a young woman I did not know. I stopped to speak to them. Aunt Fanny introduced me to her long-time friend, Frances. This appeared to be a rare time when she did not have scores of people around her. They both seemed pleased to dialogue with me for a few minutes. I told Aunt Fanny about the chapel on "holiness" and the longing I possessed to live more like our Lord. I explained that I stopped by on my way to the Communication Car. At one point I asked her if she could say anything today directly to The Prince, what would it be? She thought for a moment and then replied:

"I am Thine, O Lord, I have heard Thy voice, and it told Thy love to me; But I long to rise in the arms of faith and be closer drawn to Thee.

Draw me nearer, nearer blessed Lord, to the cross where Thou hast died; Draw me nearer, nearer, nearer blessed Lord, to Thy precious bleeding side.

Oh, the pure delight of a single hour, that before Thy throne I spend; When I kneel in prayer and with Thee, my God, I commune as friend with Friend.

There are depths of love that I cannot know, till I cross the narrow sea; There are heights of joy that I may not reach, till I rest in peace with Thee."[275]

I marveled at the beauty of her eloquent response. If Aunt Fanny longed to be nearer to The Prince, how much closer should I strive to be near Him as well? Her young friend, Frances, also spoke wisely and at one point I posed the same question to her. What would her prayer be to The Conductor's Son if she could only speak to Him once more?

She replied:

"Take my life and let it be, consecrated, Lord, to Thee; Take my moments and my days, let them flow in endless praise.

Take my hands and let them move, at the impulse of Thy love; Take my feet and let them be, swift and beautiful for Thee.

Take my voice and let me sing, always, only for my King; Take my lips and let them be, filled with messages from Thee.

Take my silver and my gold, not a mite would I withhold; Take my intellect and use, every power as Thou shalt choose.

Take my will and make it Thine, it shall be no longer mine; Take my heart, it is Thine own, it shall be Thy royal throne.

Take my love, my Lord, I pour, at Thy feet its treasure store; Take myself and I will be, ever, only, all for Thee."[276]

Young Frances' answer spoke of presenting our entire bodies to the Lord for His purpose and glory. I recalled some of the passages the porter read from The Schedule this morning in the Lord's Day Chapel highlighted this wonderful truth.[277] Soon after, I thanked the ladies for this conversation, and I proceeded to the Communication Car. As I arrived, Sarah Adams walked past me on her way out. She did not seem to notice me because I heard her whisper as she left:

"Nearer, my God, to Thee, nearer to Thee..."[278]

The same word "Nearer" came from Aunt Fanny's voice just a little while earlier. Before I began calling on The Conductor, I decided to check in on a couple of others who also came to converse with Him. I listened in on a spiritual man I knew as James Orr. He passionately poured his heart out in earnest prayer:

> "*Search me, Oh God, and know my heart today, Try me, Oh Savior, know my thoughts, I pray. See if there be some wicked way in me, Cleanse me from every sin and set me free.*"[279]

The Shepherd-Singer in Israel made a similar petition in The Schedule.[280] I lost track of how many times I prayed such a prayer myself. When I pressed the # 2 button, I heard a man I did not know. The screen identified him as Justin Van de Venter. He evidently reached a pivotal point in his experience with The Conductor:

> "*All to Jesus I surrender, all to Him I freely give; I will ever love and trust Him, in His presence daily live.*
>
> *I surrender all, I surrender all; All to Thee, my blessed Savior, I surrender all.*"[281]

The simplicity of surrender – yet how I often resisted it.

I checked in on one other passenger in the Communication Car. When I punched button # 3, I recognized Charles Tindley. I engaged in previous discussions with him on the train. Now he reached victory with The Conductor:

> "*Nothing between my soul and the Savior, naught of this world's delusive dream; I have renounced all sinful pleasure, Jesus is mine, there's nothing between.*
>
> *Nothing between my soul and the Savior, so that His blessed face may be seen; Nothing preventing the least of His favor, keep the way clear, let nothing between.*

Nothing between, like worldly pleasure, habits of life, though harmless they seem; Must not my heart from Him ever sever, He is my all, there's nothing between."[282]

I wanted that testimony! The Scriptures from The Schedule and these sayings from the saints made it easy for me to call on The Conductor. Cleansing, consecration, and correction all converged on my soul through this wonderful pathway of prayer.

The clock now showed 7 p.m. and I realized I had eaten very little on this day. I proceeded to the Dining Car to partake of something light for dinner. Every table appeared occupied. I turned to leave; however, a dark-skinned gentleman of great distinction motioned for me to come and join him. He introduced himself as Charles P. Jones. I found out later he served The Prince as a leader over many local churches. We shared a wonderful conversation, as well as a delicious meal. Brother Jones told me that another man planned to join him, however, this un-named brother canceled the appointment so he could spend more time talking to The Conductor. He showed me the note this fellow sent to him that ended:

"Just a closer walk with Thee, grant it Jesus, is my plea; Daily walking close to Thee, let it be, dear Lord, let it be."[283]

I rehearsed much of what I heard that day to Brother Jones. Several themes flowed together, such as "draw me nearer," a "closer walk," and even "higher ground" that my mentor, Johnson Oatman previously told me about. This church leader concurred with all of this, then indicated that I should also go deeper in the Faith:

"Deeper, deeper in the love of Jesus, daily let me go; Higher, higher in the school of wisdom, more of grace to show.

Oh, deeper yet I pray, and higher every day; And wiser, blessed Lord, in Thy precious, holy Word.

Deeper, deeper, blessed Holy Spirit, take me deeper still; Till my life is wholly lost in Jesus, and His perfect will.

Deeper, deeper though it cost hard trials, deeper let me go; Rooted in the holy love of Jesus, let me fruitful grow.

Deeper, higher, every day in Jesus, till all conflict past; Finds me conqueror and in His own image, perfected at last."[284]

We did not share this meal together by chance. I sensed My Companion arranged it all for me. I thanked Brother Jones for his kindness and wisdom. I wished I could have spent more time with him on the train.

After the meal I decided to go and ride for a while in the Coach Car. I often did this to reflect on the day before retiring for the night. I sat alone in the darkened passenger car, peering out the window and thinking of all the scenes and sounds a single day provided me. I pulled the card out of my pocket that the porter gave me from Mr. Longstaff. I held it up to a faint light from the window. I used it as a check list. "Speak often with the Lord" – check. "Feed on His Word" – check. "Make friends of God's children" – check. "Help those who are weak" – room for much improvement in that area. I still relied heavily on others, yet I knew I needed to be serving in some ministry for seeking souls. That time came not far in the future. I then read again the last line from Mr. Longstaff's pen:

"By looking to Jesus, like Him thou shalt be; Thy friends in thy conduct His likeness shall see."[285]

I recalled what a porter said in the chapel service earlier today, that true holiness consists of belonging to The Prince and becoming like The Prince.[286] Just then my thoughts met interruption at the sound of two voices in conversation in the seat diagonal from mine. I think others sat with them, however, I never heard anyone else speak. Since no one else sat in the Coach Car, I easily could hear the dialogue of the people who slipped into those seats. I recognized the first voice. It belonged to A.B. Simpson, another prominent leader in the church. The lady who responded to him bore the name Eliza Hewitt. I am not sure how their interaction began, but I heard the scholarly Simpson say:

> "*Once it was the blessing, now it is the Lord, Once it was the feeling, now it is His Word; Once His gift I wanted, now the Giver own, Once I sought for healing, now Himself alone.*
>
> *All in all forever, only Christ I'll sing; Everything is in Christ, and Christ is everything.*"[287]

I marveled as the man spoke with such discernment. While he continued to speak, my mind flashed forward to what The Prince meant to me. Then Eliza Hewitt answered him as if she lifted her words right out of my heart:

> "*More about Jesus would I know, more of His grace to others show; More of His saving fulness see, more of His love who died for me.*
>
> *More about Jesus let me learn, more of His holy will discern; Spirit of God my teacher be, showing the things of Christ to me.*
>
> *More about Jesus in His Word, holding communion with my Lord; Hearing His voice in every line, making each faithful saying mine.*
>
> *More about Jesus on His throne, riches in glory all His own; More of His kingdom's sure increase, more of His coming, Prince of Peace.*"[288]

Tears swelled up within my eyes as I then rode along in silent darkness. All I could say was "Amen." Marking my day as now complete, I arose and headed for my berth in the Sleeping Car. I happened to pass by an acquaintance named Lee Roy Abernathy in the corridor. I shared with him my heart's desire to draw closer to The Prince. He agreed, saying:

> "I want to know more about my Lord."[289]

We prayed for each other then I retired for the evening, grateful that I could keep growing in grace and thankful I could do so with others. Sleep did not come easy to me that night. As I was tossing and turning in my berth, I heard someone nearby crying out to The Conductor. This person evidently turned his or her bed into an altar. As I listened intently, I could hear some of their Evening Prayer:

> *"If I have wounded any soul today, If I have caused one foot to go astray; If I have walked in my own willful way, Dear Lord, forgive!*
>
> *If I have uttered idle words or vain, If I have turned aside from want or pain, Lest I myself shall suffer through the strain, Dear Lord, forgive!*
>
> *Forgive the sins I have confessed to Thee, Forgive the secret sins I do not see; O guide me, love me, and my Keeper be, Dear Lord, forgive!"*[290]

I repeated the closing stanzas of that prayer, not only that night, but all the remaining evenings on my journey aboard the *Ecclesia Express*.

Chapter Twelve –
PRAYER

I met several passengers on the *Ecclesia Express* whose relationship with The Prince appeared to be much closer than mine. Some of these saints seemed to live exclusively from "glory to glory" as it says somewhere in The Schedule.[291]

For example, I rode with a group of such overcomers in the Coach Car for many miles one afternoon. There were three men and two women seated with me in our compartment. They included Brother J.E. French, Brother William Hunter, and Brother C. Austin Miles. The two ladies were Sister Anne Cousin and Miriam Oatman, the daughter of my mentor, Johnson Oatman.

These followers of The Prince lived in such victory they sometimes likened their present experience to life in the Shining City. For example, midway through our time together the conversation turned to the wonders of the Christian life. Anne Cousin, the brilliant writer in our midst, also proved an effective speaker when she eloquently stated:

"The sands of time are sinking, the dawn of Heaven breaks, the summer morn I've sighed for, the fair, sweet morn awakes; Dark, dark hath

been the midnight, but dayspring is at hand, And glory, glory dwelleth, in Immanuel's Land.

The Bride eyes not her garment, but her dear Bridegroom's face, I will not gaze at glory, but on my King of grace; Not at the crown He giveth, but on His pierced hand,

The Lamb is all the glory, of Immanuel's Land."[292]

William Hunter, a minister in his own right, continued that line of thought:

"I am dwelling on the mountain, where the golden sunlight gleams, o'er a land whose wondrous beauty, far exceeds my fondest dreams.

Is not this the land of Beulah? Blessed, blessed land of light; Where the flowers bloom forever, and the sun is always bright.

Tell me not of heavy crosses, nor of burdens hard to bear, For I've found this great salvation, makes each burden light appear.

And I love to follow Jesus, gladly counting all but dross, Worldly honors all forsaking, for the glory of the cross."[293]

Brother Miles previously shared with me about the Risen Prince and testified on the day I returned from Calvary. Now he echoed the same sentiment concerning living in what they called "Beulah Land:"

"I'm living on the mountain underneath a cloudless sky, I'm drinking at the fountain that never shall run dry; O yes, I'm feasting on the manna from a bountiful supply, For I am dwelling in Beulah Land.

Let the stormy breezes blow, their cry cannot alarm me, I am safely sheltered here, protected by God's hand; Here the sun is always shining, here there's naught can harm me, I am safe forever in Beulah Land."[294]

I knew that some of the porters on occasion would refer to the Shining City as being in Canaan Land or Beulah Land. However, I remember reading in The Schedule about battles to win and giants to overcome in the original promised land.[295] I assumed these saints were talking about the victories of the sanctified life. Young Miriam Oatman shared her testimony:

"I was once in Egypt's bondage, but deliverance came to me; And I'm living now in Canaan, for the Son hath made me free.

I am living now in Canaan, Jesus' blood avails for me; I am free from condemnation, for the Son hath made me free."[296]

Finally, Brother French spoke up. He displayed silence during the lively discussion about the triumphant life promised for those who follow The Prince. He then concurred with the others:

"We find many people who can't understand why we are so happy and free, we've crossed over Jordan to Canaan's fair land, and this is like Heaven to me.

So when we are happy, we sing and we shout, some don't understand us, you see; We're filled with the Spirit, there is not a doubt, and this is like Heaven to me.

We've heard the sweet music, the heavenly chord, from glory land over the sea; A soul-thrilling message from Jesus our Lord, and this is like Heaven to me.

We're looking for Jesus with glory to come, 'tis Jesus Who died on the tree; A cloud of bright angels to carry me home, O that will be Heaven for me."[297]

A short time later our group disbursed, with some going to the Dining Car and others back to their sleeping berths. This group mirrored so many passengers on the train who made me love The Conductor, The Prince, My Companion, The Schedule, the porters, and the other passengers more – just by being in their presence. They did not make themselves appear to be better, nor did they make me and others to feel inferior. They made me long for the Shining City and inspired me to live closer to Jesus, The Crown Prince of Calvary.

I must confess, however, that my life did not consist of only sunshine and roses. Despite growing in the grace and knowledge of our Prince, I also experienced struggles along my journey.[298] These included bouts of loneliness, for I did not have a close, personal, friend. These instances would intensify when I became tired or had not eaten properly. I also faced financial concerns, for like most of the passengers, we still worked for an income even while traveling on the train. Worst of all, despite not wanting to wind up back in sin, from time to time I would slip, stumble, fall, or fail. At one particularly low moment in my Christian life, I sought the counsel from one of the trusted porters on board. He encouraged me to intensify my prayer life. He instructed me to set aside a certain time in the evening for one entire week to come to the Communication Car to converse with The Conductor. He arranged to have a different prayer partner meet with me each night – and they did.

I met with these mentors one-on-one each evening at 7:30 p.m. They challenged me with an admonition concerning my prayer life and then I would go into the Communication Car for an extended time of talking to The Conductor. On Monday, I met with Edmund Lorenz. He proved to be a good choice for the first night. He asked me a series of questions that all were on target:

> "*Are you weary, are you heavy-hearted? Tell it to Jesus, Tell it to Jesus. Are you grieving over joys departed? Tell it to Jesus alone.*
>
> *Do the tears flow down your cheeks unbidden? Tell it to Jesus, Tell it to Jesus. Have you sins that to men's eyes are hidden? Tell it to Jesus alone.*
>
> *Do you fear the gathering clouds of sorrow? Tell it to Jesus, Tell it to Jesus. Are you anxious what shall be tomorrow? Tell it to Jesus alone.*
>
> *Are you troubled at the thought of dying? Tell it to Jesus, Tell it to Jesus. For Christ's coming kingdom are you sighing? Tell it to Jesus alone.*"[299]

And that is what I did in the conversation booth. I knew that The Conductor, the great Engineer, already knew what I was facing and thinking, but I told Him all from the depths of my heart any way.[300] On Tuesday evening the porter arranged for Elisha Hoffman to meet with me. We were not strangers to each other. He had asked if I had been washed in the blood of the Lamb after the chapel service before I stopped at Calvary. He also testified at the party when we returned from the cross. I welcomed seeing him again. He knew what Edmund Lorenz had told me last night and he took it a step further, sharing with me about a personal time in his own life when he felt a divine compulsion to spend critical time in prayer. He indicated I needed to follow through with this same passionate petition:

"*I must tell Jesus all of my trials, I cannot bear these burdens alone; In my distress He kindly will help me, He ever loves and cares for His own.*

I must tell Jesus! I must tell Jesus! I cannot bear these burdens alone; I must tell Jesus! I must tell Jesus! Jesus can help me, Jesus alone.

I must tell Jesus all of my troubles, He is a kind, compassionate Friend; If I but ask Him, He will deliver, make of my troubles quickly an end."[301]

I took heart that someone else felt like I did. Burdens, trials, and troubles were never meant to be borne alone. The Prince welcomed us to tell Him the deepest hurts of our heart.

Wednesday night's mentor was a poet named Joseph Scriven. His counsel also focused on The Prince as the best of friends in which to confide in:

"*What a friend we have in Jesus, all our sins and griefs to bear, what a privilege to carry, everything to God in prayer.*

O what peace we often forfeit, O what needless pain we bear, all because we do not carry, everything to God in prayer.

Have we trials and temptations, is there trouble anywhere, we should never be discouraged, take it to the Lord in prayer.

Can we find a friend so faithful, who will all our sorrows share? Jesus knows our every weakness, take it to the Lord in prayer."[302]

I had never considered all the benefits and blessings that we sometimes fail to receive simply because we do not engage in meaningful conversations with The Conductor. I remember a porter saying once that things happen when people pray that would not have happened unless they prayed. Like the two nights before, the Wednesday session with The Conductor in the communication booth proved fulfilling. On Thursday, two mentors showed up, which greatly surprised me. The first, a lady named Annie Hawkes, accompanied a man named Ray Palmer. They each taught me the same thing about talking to The Prince in two different ways. She gave me this sample prayer:

"I need Thee every hour, most gracious Lord; No tender voice like Thine can peace afford... I need Thee, Oh I need Thee, every hour I need Thee; Oh bless me now, my Savior, I come to Thee."[303]

Ray Palmer's comments included this expression:

"My faith looks up to Thee, Thou Lamb of Calvary, Savior divine! Now hear me while I pray, take all my guilt away, Oh, let me from this day, be wholly Thine."[304]

Annie Hawkes knew the truth. I not only needed The Prince when in trouble; I needed Him every hour of every day. I kept Ray Palmer's closing sentence in my heart for a long time. The guilt of past failures, both before and after I visited Calvary plagued me too long "From this day on" assured me that even though I could not have a totally new beginning, I could indeed script a new end to my life. On Friday evening, I met with a Mr. William Walford for our discussion before the dialogue with The Conductor. As a minister, he dispensed much wisdom to me. He emphasized the value of these moments spent with the Master. It quickly became clear that he greatly anticipated without dread each time he could converse with the Lord himself:

"Sweet hour of prayer! Sweet hour of prayer! That calls me from a world of care, and bids me at my Father's throne, makes all my wants and wishes known;

In seasons of distress and grief, my soul has often found relief, and oft escaped the tempter's snare, by thy return, sweet hour of prayer."[305]

I experienced a most wonderful time of conversation with The Conductor that night. When I walked out of the Communication Car, I felt surprised to see William Walford waiting for me. He felt inclined to share one more admonition with me. It concerned being faithful in these conversations until our journey on this train reached completion. He worded it this way:

"Sweet hour of prayer! Sweet hour of prayer! May I thy consolation share, Till from Mount Pisgah's lofty height, I view my home and take my flight;

This robe of flesh I'll drop and rise, to seize the everlasting prize, and shout, while passing through the air, 'Farewell, farewell, sweet hour of prayer."[306]

What imagery to illustrate his point! I knew from The Schedule that Mount Pisgah became the place where Moses looked over and saw the promised land.[307] Just as sure that he saw the land of his dreams, so also will we when the train pulls into the station at the Shining City. When we drop the garments of mortality that we have been wearing, we will put on immortality. In my mind I pictured what Brother Walford suggested – that, as we are exiting the train and rising to our reward, we will turn around and shout "Good-bye" to these sweet hours of conversation with the King. We will not need to pray in that eternal city because we will be in the very presence of our Lord forever! I headed for my berth in the Sleeping Car so thankful for the first five nights of this week.

While waiting for my mentor to arrive on Saturday evening a little after 7:00 p.m., I wondered who it would be. I felt great delight when I saw

Charles Tindley coming to meet with me. He was a man of color, but even more obvious, a man of convictions. I first met him on the caboose back before Calvary when he shared with another brother that "We will understand it better by and by." I also had ridden part of the journey with him in the Coach Car after I had been to Calvary. I remember that he ended our discussion that day by praying to The Prince in a powerful way:

> "When the storms of life are raging, stand by me, When the storms of life are raging, stand by me.
>
> When the world is tossing me, like a ship upon the sea, Thou who rulest wind and water, stand by me.
>
> In the midst of tribulation, stand by me, In the midst of tribulation, stand by me;
>
> When the hosts of hell assail, and my strength begins to fail, Thou who never lost a battle, stand by me.
>
> When I'm growing old and feeble, stand by me, When I'm growing old and feeble, stand by me.
>
> When my life becomes a burden, and I'm nearing chilly Jordan, O Thou Lily of the Valley, stand by me."[308]

Charles Tindley not only knew about prayer, he, himself, knew how to pray. I shared with him some of my struggles, especially my long history of carrying extra baggage with me. He instructed me to leave every burden with The Conductor, just as I had done with all my sins when I met The Prince at Calvary.[309] Our time together rapidly took wings and flew by. As we parted I turned to enter the Communication Car and he stopped and raised his hand and told me to remember not to carry a single burden away from The Conductor when my time with Him was over:

> "Leave it there, leave it there, Take your burden to the Lord and leave it there; If you trust and never doubt, He will surely bring you out.
>
> Take your burden to the Lord and leave it there.

If the world from you withhold of its silver and its gold, and you have to get along with meager fare; Just remember in His Word, how He feeds the little bird.

Take your burden to the Lord and leave it there.

If your body suffers pain and your health you can't regain, and your soul is almost sinking in despair, Jesus knows the pain you feel, He can save and He can heal.

Take your burden to the Lord and leave it there.

When your youthful days are gone and old age is stealing on, and your body bends beneath the weight of care; He will never leave you then, He'll go with you to the end.

Take your burden to the Lord and leave it there."[310]

That Saturday night proved to be a milestone moment in my quest to serve The Prince with honor. I did not know it then, but My Companion had saved the best for Sunday. The exuberant preacher - evangelist Vep Ellis met me in front of the Communication Car for my final mentor session. He likely did not remember me, but I remembered him. He talked to me about the love of God on my very first night aboard the train. This longtime minister emphasized my need for persistence in prayer and making sure The Conductor had blessed me in order that I, in turn, could bless others. He explained it this way:

"Let me touch Him, let me touch Jesus, let me touch Him as He passes by; Then when I shall reach out to others, they shall know Him, they shall live, and not die.

Oh to be His hand extended, reaching out to the oppressed; Let me touch Him, let me touch Jesus, so that others may know and be blessed."[311]

When our dialogue concluded, I thanked Brother Ellis and went into the Communication Car. This time of intersession with The Conductor again produced much fruit. It seems I drew strength from all the teaching

I received that week and it flowed together in a special way. The Prince provided assurance that some of my heaviest burdens were being lifted and some of my lingering questions were being answered. To my surprise, when I emerged from the prayer chamber, I saw Brother Ellis again. He had followed me into the chamber and engaged in his own conversation with The Conductor. I shared with him my perceived victories in prayer, and he expressed that he himself had prevailed in petitioning The Prince, in accordance with His will. His testimony thrilled my own soul:

> *"The clouds have passed away, I see the light of day, The sun is shining through, dispelling gloom with hallelujahs; I know that this is real, for in my heart I feel, that my Savior heard my earnest prayer.*
>
> *When in the future days, the fiery trials blaze, When Satan comes to me to take away my victory; I can point him to the time when Heaven's light did shine, I can say He heard my earnest prayer.*
>
> *I know He heard my prayer, He knows my every care, He gives to me the blessed victory; O yes, I feel Him now, my loyalty I vow, I know the Savior heard my plea.*
>
> *The enemy had said that my faith in God was dead, and if the way was rough, He did not care; Thank God, it is not true, He thrills me through and through, I know the Savior heard my* prayer."[312]

The Evangelist Vep Ellis proved to be a predictive prophet in this area of my life. The days and weeks ahead included times when the Tempter came up to me and mocked my dependence upon The Conductor and our conversations together. He implied such dialogues functioned only as a waste of time. However, I boldly pointed back to every night of this special week and told him that he came too late to change my mind – The Prince had already done the work in my life.

Chapter Thirteen –
SOUL WINNING

My life certainly underwent a dramatic change since I took the trip to Calvary. Before that transforming event, I got off at almost every stop along the journey and usually came back to the train with my arms filled with more baggage that I did not need. As I grew in my faith as a believer, I had less and less desires for the things available at the stops along the way. My greatest passion became knowing more about The Beloved Prince who had given His life for me. I loved to spend hours reading, studying, memorizing, and meditating on many parts of The Schedule. Spending time with fellow passengers of like precious faith became a source of great joy. My likes and dislikes had been completely rearranged as the *Ecclesia Express* became my "second home."

However, over time something began to bother me. I noticed several of my fellow passengers would get off the train at every stop. I wondered why they were doing this. Surely the Tempter did not entice them to adapt more of the world's systems into their life? Not in the least. I soon found out the reason they were exiting the train. They did so to bring other people on board so they too might experience salvation at Calvary. One of the porters explained this to me when he showed me in The Schedule about the Great Confession, the Great Commandment, and the Great Commission.[313] I stood in complete agreement with the ancient apostle in his Great Confession that The Prince was indeed the "Christ, the Son of the living God." Likewise, I tried my best to love The Mighty Conductor with all my being and other people as well. (The Engineer was always easy to love; some people remain easier to love if they are a great distance away!) It was the Great Commission – the Savior's command for us to go and make disciples of all people – that I fell far short on.

I certainly knew that the lost world needed to be saved. I somehow felt that the responsibility to reach them belonged to only "special-called" passengers. However, during a meal with a half dozen people seated around the table, a woman named Kittie Suffield said something that convicted my soul:

> "In the harvest field now ripened, there's a work for us all to do; Hark the voice of God is calling, hear Him calling, calling you.
>
> Does the place you're called to labor, seem so small and little known; It is great if God is in it, and He'll not forsake His own.
>
> When the conflict here is ended, and our race on earth is run; He will say if we are faithful, come my child, you've made it home.
>
> Little is much when God is in it, labor not for wealth or fame; There's a crown and you can win it, if you'll go in Jesus' name."[314]

Several of us seated at that scene confessed that we felt inadequate for the Lord to use us in such a personal, important way. This conversation represented the first stirrings of my heart to replace my "omission" with His "commission." As always, Aunt Fanny also had words that seemed especially designed for me. As we left the Dining Car, I heard her sharing with a group around her:

> "Rescue the perishing, care for the dying, Snatch them in pity from sin and the grave; Weep o'er the erring one, lift up the fallen, tell them of Jesus, the mighty to save.

Though they are slighting Him, still He is waiting, Waiting the penitent child to receive; Plead with them earnestly, plead with them gently, He will forgive if they only believe.

Down in the human heart, crushed by the tempter, Feelings lie buried that grace can restore; Touched by a loving heart, wakened by kindness, chords that were broken will vibrate once more.

Rescue the perishing, duty demands it, Strength for thy labor the Lord will provide; Back to the narrow way patiently win them, tell the poor wanderer a Savior has died.

Rescue the perishing, care for the dying; Jesus is merciful, Jesus will save."[315]

Tears filled my eyes as I felt my heart breaking for the plight of lost men and women. How could I have forgotten that I too existed in such a condition. I retreated to my space in the Sleeping Car and passed the next couple of days with weeping for the souls unprepared for the Shining City. I knew I must become more involved in the rescue efforts for The Prince of Peace. Upon further inquiry, I learned that soul winning activity involved more than only selected individuals. On the contrary, the train conducted an organized operation of rescuers being dispatched at every locomotive stop. One of the porters pointed me to the lounge area when we were less than an hour away from a scheduled stop. Upon arrival, I found a woman and a man carrying on a conversation while training about a dozen other people. The lady, with the last name of Thomas, quizzed the gentleman and the others:

"Hark! 'tis the Shepherd's voice I hear, out in the desert dark and drear; Calling the sheep who've gone astray, far from the Shepherd's fold away.

Bring them in, bring them in, Bring them in from the fields of sin; Bring them in, bring them in, Bring the wandering ones to Jesus.

Who'll go and help this Shepherd kind, help Him the wandering ones to find; Who'll bring the lost ones to the fold, where they'll be sheltered from the cold?"[316]

All the listeners raised their hands in response to her questions as Mr. Shaw provided the verbal reply:

"Sowing in the morning, sowing seeds of kindness, sowing in the noontide and the dewy eve; Waiting for the harvest, and the time of reaping, we shall come rejoicing, bringing in the sheaves."[317]

A porter read from some of the songs listed in The Schedule and the group prayed together before leaving the train when it came to a stop.[318] No one went out alone, rather, they were sent two-by-two.[319] One person prepared to share the truth of The Prince's salvation, while the partner took care of removing distractions and lending whatever support deemed necessary. As I saw this group of trained workers exit the train, I felt My Companion nudging me toward this kind of ministry. That night, I laid awake for hours asking The Conductor for guidance in how to best win others to Him. I kept thinking about Brother Shaw's goal from the song: to be able to have sheaves in my hand to lay at The Prince's feet when this life is over. From far back in my memory I recalled a man named Charles who wrestled with this same issue:

"Must I go and empty-handed, thus my dear Redeemer meet? Not one day of service give Him, lay no trophy at His feet?

Must I go and empty-handed, must I meet my Savior so; Not one soul with which to greet Him, must I empty-handed go?"[320]

There in the darkness on my bed I made a vow to The Prince that I would win someone to Him. Like the ancient apostle, I knew I could not win them all, but I felt equally sure that I could win some.[321]

The next morning, I arose early and went to The Conductor's Car to speak more to the Great Engineer. When I slipped into a booth and heard other conversations with Him, I felt pleased to know that fellow passengers were making similar commitments. I listened in on a woman named Mary Brown:

> *"I'll go where You want me to go, dear Lord, o'er mountain or plain or sea; I'll say what You want me to say, dear Lord, I'll be what You want me to be."*[322]

I felt blessed that C. Austin Miles stopped by to speak to me for a moment. He had become a trusted friend that I turned to for guidance at various times. He shared this sentiment with me:

> *"It is not mine to question the judgment of my Lord, it is but mine to follow the leadings of His Word. But if to go or stay, or whether here or there, I'll be, with my Savior, content anywhere.*
>
> *If Jesus goes with me, I'll go anywhere, 'Tis Heaven to me, where'er I may be, if He is there. I count it a privilege here, His cross to bear, If Jesus goes with me, I'll go anywhere."*[323]

That word "go" continued to echo in my spirit. We must "come to Him" for rest and drink, but then "go for Him" to win others for the Shining City.[324] I clicked on another screen and was surprised to see a young fiery follower of The Prince named Nancy Harmon. (I remembered meeting her a few years before this dream.) She, too, expressed her willingness to carry the Good News to those who needed to hear it:

> *"If you need a voice to speak for You, I'll speak, if you need someone to weep for souls, I'll weep; If I see You've got a job to do, then I'll work Lord anytime for You, though it may be morning, night or noon – I'll go.*
>
> *I'll go, I'll go, Anytime, anyplace, to any creature of any race; To the mountains, through the valleys, cross the river, through heat or cold, Anywhere You lead me Lord, I'll go."*[325]

To hear so many others responding to the call strengthened the commitment I made in my own life. I determined to join the rescue operation when they assembled prior to the next stop. I possessed numerous things I needed to overcome – inadequacies real and imagined. I used many excuses for not being active in the winning of souls. One of which included my lack of knowing The Schedule as good as I should have. I was afraid that someone would ask me questions that I did not know the answer. The porters assured me that there existed four primary truths to remember when telling others about The Prince.[326] First, all humanity remains lost and undone without His salvation. Second, consequences must be faced if we remain lost. Third, The Prince accomplished something for us (dying and rising) so we do not have to remain lost, and fourth, we must do something in response to His redemptive acts (believe and repent). The porters suggested that I take the subordinate role as the assisting partner on my first soul winning endeavor. This I did while teamed with Brother William Ogden. This evangelist knew a powerful way to deliver the message. I heard him share this with several people:

> *"'Tis the grandest theme, let the tidings roll, to the guilty heart, to the sinful soul; Look to God in faith, He will make thee whole, our God is able to deliver thee.*
>
> *He is able to deliver thee, He is able to deliver thee; Though by sin oppressed, go to Him for rest, Our God is able to deliver thee."*[327]

As was true with the Apostle Paul, we did not win them all, but we did win some. In time I was able to take the lead role in witnessing to others. One of the porters helped me gain confidence to do this by exhorting me to simply share my personal testimony to lost people.[328] I had certainly told my story to several individuals. However, they were all faithful followers of The Prince and passengers on the train. The porter instructed me to remember three words: "Before," "How," and "Since." He said to simply fill in the blanks to "Before I met The Prince, my life___" "How I met The Prince___" and "Since I met The Prince, my life___" He assured me that every believer has a testimony, whether they were raised in a Christian home or if they had a dramatic conversion. Soon after, I was walking through the Coach Car, when I saw Mr. Albert Brumley. He was sitting in his usual place on the train – out of the spotlight in the corner away from the traffic. On the spot, I asked him about his personal testimony. He replied:

"Once like a bird in prison I dwelt, no freedom from my sorrow I felt;
But Jesus came and listened to me and glory to God, He set me free.

He set me free, yes, He set me free, He broke the bonds of prison for me;
I'm glory bound my Jesus to see, for glory to God, He set me free.

Now I am climbing higher each day, darkness of night has drifted away;
My feet are planted on higher ground, and glory to God, I'm homeward bound."[329]

And there it was! "Before…," "How…," and "Since…." I began to ask many people on the train to share their personal testimony with me. Each one of them had these three distinct parts clearly audible. One that stood out to me came from a brother named Henry Zelley. Here is how he responded to my question:

"My heart was distressed 'neath Jehovah's dread frown, and low in the pit where my sins dragged me down.

I cried to the Lord from the deep miry clay, who tenderly brought me out to golden day.

He brought me out of the miry clay, He set my feet on the Rock to stay;
He puts a song in my soul today, A song of praise, Hallelujah!

He gave me a song, 'twas a new song of praise, By day and by night its sweet notes I will raise.

My heart's overflowing, I'm happy and free, I'll praise my Redeemer Who has rescued me.

I'll sing of His wonderful mercy to me, I'll praise Him till all men His goodness shall see.

I'll sing of salvation at home and abroad, till many shall hear the truth and trust in God."[330]

Once again "Before...," "How...," and "Since..." were clearly stated and distinguished.

I must confess that, despite my stated intentions and vows to The Prince, I found myself often neglecting to share the truth about Christ with those who needed Him. I possessed great confidence while on the train, but my courage often turned to cowardice when I got off at one of the stops. Something missing in my life flourished in the first passengers that ever rode on the *Ecclesia Express*.[331] A porter pointed out to me that the final words The Prince spoke to us before He ascended to the Shining City included the promise of power after the Holy Spirit came upon us.[332] The boldness of believers caused the train to be filled in the earliest years.[333]

Not long after on a Sunday night, the Lounge Car was closed to all except those who wanted to come together and seek The Conductor for more courage to speak for Him. I heard they thought the Communication Car might not be able to hold all the people. That proved correct. The Lounge filled up with hungry hearts and seeking souls, desperate for more unction and anointing for their service. A man named William Mackay led the opening prayer:

"We praise Thee, O God, for the Son of Thy love; For Jesus Who died and is now gone above; Hallelujah, Thine the glory, Hallelujah, Amen.

Hallelujah, Thine the glory, Revive us again.

Revive us again, fill each heart with Thy love, may each soul be rekindled with fire from above; Hallelujah, Thine the glory, Hallelujah, Amen.

Hallelujah, Thine the glory, Revive us again."[334]

I heard about famous revivals in history, but I sensed now, something similar happening in our own time. Suddenly a man began to cry out for what those early passengers possessed during the infant days of the divine railroad. He referenced some of the action items in The Schedule:

> *"They were in an upper chamber, they were all with one accord; When the Holy Ghost descended, as was promised by our Lord.*
>
> *O Lord, send the power just now, O Lord, send the power just now; O Lord, send the power just now, and baptize everyone.*
>
> *"Yes, this 'old time' power was given, to our fathers who were true; This is promised to believers, and we all may have it too."*[335]

I do not understand everything that happened that night – even in my own heart. I know that My Companion, the precious Spirit of God, had always been with me, even before I trusted in The Prince. I also know that He dwelt *within* me since that moment I received life at Calvary. But this night, He empowered me in such a way that provided me the boldness that I so much lacked and longed for. It was *more* of the Spirit! Not more than other people have, but more of Him than I previously had. (And hopefully He now had more of me.) A man named Frank Bottome explained it this way:

> *"O boundless love divine! How shall this tongue of mine, to wondering mortals tell the matchless grace divine;*
>
> *That I, a child of hell, should in His image shine, The Comforter has come!*
>
> *The Comforter has come, the Comforter has come! The Holy Ghost from Heaven, the Father's promise given.*
>
> *O spread the tidings 'round, wherever man is found, The Comforter has come!"*[336]

Herbert Buffum was there too. He described the scene the same way:

"He is with me everywhere and He knows my every care, I'm as happy as a bird and just as free; For the Spirit has control, Jesus satisfies my soul,

Since the Comforter abides with me."[337]

How wonderful The Prince promised to send someone to be with us just like Himself![338] I soon came to realize that I could exchange my cowardice for His courage when telling the last, the least, and the lost about The Prince of life.

One other practice on the *Ecclesia Express* became a special part of my journey to the Shining City. I attended a Lord's Day Chapel that featured the ministry of missions. The speaker, Charles Gabriel, captured my heart with his stirring presentation:

"There's a call comes ringing o'er the restless wave, 'Send the light! Send the light!' There are souls to rescue, there are souls to save, 'Send the light! Send the light!'

We have heard the Macedonian call today, 'Send the light! Send the light!' And a golden offering at the cross we lay, 'Send the light! Send the light!'

Let us pray that grace may everywhere abound, 'Send the light! Send the light' And a Christ-like spirit everywhere be found, 'Send the light! Send the light!'

Let us not grow weary in the work of love, 'Send the light! Send the light!' Let us gather jewels for a crown above, 'Send the light! Send the light!'"[339]

This marked the first time I became specifically aware that some of the Lord's servants willingly got on other trains that went in the opposite direction to take the news of The Prince to those who never heard it. (The Conductor always provided a connecting train for these loyal followers to make it to the Shining City when their summons came.) The porters in the chapel service stressed the importance of everyone being involved in the Great Commission. They said each person should either go to these unreached people or help support those who do go. I already set aside a tenth of my earnings to give to the train each week. Because I no longer desired to acquire so much excess baggage, I discovered I had funds, every month to share with those who were sending the light that Charles Gabriel talked about.[340]

Over time I eventually came to be troubled by one or two thoughts in my mind. First, I feared not doing enough for The Prince and second, not being successful in the things I did try to do for Him. My Companion used two different passengers on board to help me with these fears. I met a delightful lady named Ruth Munsey. She and her husband possessed a great passion for missions and had served The Conductor for many years. When I shared with her my angst, she replied to me:

"If I carry the gospel to the lost, near and far, I won't stand empty handed at God's judgment bar; But I dare not relax until I've done all He asks...

...lest I should leave behind an unfinished task.

When I come to the crossing, I'll be leaving behind, all my earthly possessions, and this I won't mind; It will make my heart glad, when I leave all I've had...

...if I don't leave behind an unfinished task.

You have run the race, you have kept the faith, these words I long to hear the Savior say; And when my life on earth is past, there's just one thing, dear Lord, I ask:

Don't let me leave behind an unfinished task."[341]

Her words provided me much comfort. Another wise woman, Lucie Eddie Campbell, encouraged me when I experienced repeated failures in trying to win others to The Prince. During a conversation one day in the Lounge Car she spoke this to me:

"If when you give the best of your service, telling the world that the Savior is come; Be not dismayed when men do not believe you, He understands, He'll say, 'Well done'…

But if you try and fail in your trying, hands sore and scarred from the work you've begun; Take up your cross and run quickly to meet Him, He'll understand and say, 'Well done.'

O when I come to the end of my journey, weary of life and the battle is won; Carrying the staff and the cross of redemption, He'll understand and say, 'Well done.'"[342]

I finally realized if I am somewhere serving The Prince, He will know where to find me when He comes. Finishing faithful became the goal for my remaining days.

Chapter Fourteen –

THE DEATH OF
THE SAINTS

One of the most difficult parts of this long train trip involved having to say "good-bye" to fellow passengers. At various times, many of them reached a condition where it became apparent that they were going to die before The Prince returned. In such cases, the train would make a special stop and connect with another train that would take them to the Shining City before the rest of us. On these occasions, all the passengers were invited to come to the Lounge Car and bid their farewells to the departing travel companions. One such scene stood out to me. It seems many faithful followers of The Prince received a notice that their summons to the Shining City accelerated to the present day and soon they would be placed on a special train to take them to that home.

When I arrived in the Lounge Car, several people were already present. The best chairs were reserved for those who would be transitioning to the new train. One of the porters began by reading several precious promises from The Schedule.[343] Then, as always, John Fawcett and Henry

Lyte addressed this audience. Fawcett's remarks focused on the unity of the faith:

> "*Blest be the tie that binds, our hearts in Christian love; The fellowship of kindred minds, is like to that above.*
>
> *When we asunder part, it gives us inward pain; But we shall still be joined in heart and hope to meet again.*"[344]

Brother Henry Lyte followed the opening speaker with a special prayer to The Conductor for His blessings upon those who would be leaving us soon.

> "*Abide with me; fast falls the eventide, the darkness deepens, Lord with me abide; When other helpers fail and comforts flee, Help of the helpless, oh, abide with me.*
>
> *Hold Thou Thy cross before my closing eyes, shine through the gloom and point me to the skies; Heaven's morning breaks and earth's vain shadows flee, in life, in death, O Lord, abide with me.*"[345]

The porter then explained that if any of the suffering saints would like to say a final word, they would now be permitted to do so. I knew some of those who testified, while others I met for the first time. Herbert Buffam spoke up first. He certainly was not a stranger to any of us. He had recently helped me better understand the role of My Companion – the precious Holy Spirit. Now eternity was in his sights:

> "*I've been traveling for Jesus so much of my life, I've been traveling on land and on sea; But I'm planning on taking a trip to the sky, that will be the last move for me.*
>
> *When I move to the sky, up to Heaven on high, what a wonderful trip that will be; I'm already to go, washed in Calvary's flow, that will be the last move for me.*"[346]

So many of us grew weary with the rigors of life's journey and could easily identify with the sentiments he shared. But Brother Buffam added something else. His mind certainly focused on the future inside the Shining City:

"In that city where the Lamb is the light, the city where there cometh no night; I've a mansion over there and when free from toil and care. I am going where the Lamb is the light.

There the flowers bloom forever and the day, shall be one eternal day without a night; And our tears shall be forever wiped away, in that city where the Lamb is the light."[347]

I noticed the absolute absence of any apprehension, anxiety, or fear as he faced his last days on earth. The first of many testimonies certainly resonated among us. Someone they called Daniel spoke next:

"When our days shall know their number, and in death we sweetly slumber, When the King commands the spirit to be free; Nevermore with anguish laden, we shall reach that lovely Eden when they ring the golden bells for you and me."[348]

This brother proceeded to tell what he believed awaited him. He called it a *"glory hallelujah Jubilee."* At that moment James Rowe stepped forward. He had become a trusted friend on the journey since we shared a meal together, even before I expressed my devotion to The Prince. I was delighted to see him on this occasion and to hear him speak:

"After the midnight morning will greet us, after the sadness, joy will appear; After the tempest, sunlight will meet us, after the jeering, praise we shall hear.

After the battle, peace will be given, after the weeping, song there will be; After the journey there will be Heaven, burdens will fall and we will be free.

Shadows and sunshine all through the story, teardrops and pleasure day after day; But when we reach the kingdom of glory, trials of earth will vanish away.

After the shadows there will be sunshine, after the frown, the soul-cheering smile;

Cling to the Savior, love Him forever, all will be well in a little while."[349]

His words resonated with all who heard them. The thought of the destination caused James Rowe to ask:

"Won't it be Wonderful There?"[350]

The Prince prompted the start of our journey and He likewise remained paramount at the end for these saints nearing the shores of the Shining City. A porter then read part of the story from The Schedule about the rich lost man and poor saved man that The Prince told us about while He was on earth.[351] The former died and went to Hell, while angels came and gathered the latter man to his eternal reward. The next speaker, identified as Jefferson Hascall, must have had that in his mind as he shared his personal testimony:

"My latest sun is sinking fast, my race is nearly run; My strongest trials now are past, my triumph has begun.

I know I'm near the holy ranks, of friends and kindred dear; I hear the waves of Jordan's banks, the crossing must be near.

I've almost reached my heavenly home, my spirit loudly sings; Thy holy ones, behold they come, I hear the noise of wings.

Oh bear my longing heart to Him, who bled and died for me; Whose blood now cleanses from all sin and gives me victory.

O come, angel band, Come and around me stand."[352]

As this gentleman continued to speak, my mind drifted to what that must be like – to realize the short distance to the heavenly home and the

Savior who purchased our ticket! And then I wondered if perhaps I could be closer to the crossing than what I presumed. Thomas Ramsey stood to speak as the last traveler to share his closing testimony with the group. His words touched us all as he said:

"I won't have to cross Jordan alone."[353]

The last grace gift for the Conductor's children occurs when the blessed Companion shows up at the final river and escorts them into the presence of The Prince. The porter then asked if any of the remaining passengers had any further words of encouragement for those getting ready to take the final train to the Shining City. Mr. Gilmore immediately stood up. I remembered him as one of the encouragers during our discussion on suffering some months before. He must have been greatly impacted by all the references to the Jordan River as an imagery of death. He passionately moved the crowd with these words:

"And when my task on earth is done, when by Thy grace the victory's won; In death's cold wave I will not flee, since God through Jordan leadeth me."[354]

Everyone there, those going and those staying, all nodded in agreement and said "Amen." At this moment a hush grew over those crowded into the car because a porter asked a guest to lead in a special prayer. As we all bowed our heads, Augustus Toplady stepped forward and began to address the invisible Conductor. He concluded his prayer with these words:

"While I draw this fleeting breath, when mine eyes shall close in death, When I rise to worlds unknown, and behold Thee on Thy throne. Rock of Ages, cleft for me, let me hide myself in Thee. "[355]

I had never met the man, nor did I know he was on this train. I had heard of him, and I made a pledge to myself to never forget the words of his prayer.

Again, the guests expressed their gratitude for such admonitions. An ardent follower of Jesus, Esther Rusthoi, moved to worship in anticipation of beholding The Prince soon. She captured the feelings of us all by saying:

"It will be worth it all, when we see Jesus."[356]

At that moment, the train began to slow down and soon would stop with a screeching halt. The porter declared that the time to say good-byes arrived. The passengers began to hug one another and whisper their farewells to their long-time friends. Some husbands and wives were exchanging final words, the same with parents and children, siblings, and families of every relation. Tears began to flow as promises for a future reunion rang out. One said to another:

"Yes, we'll gather at the river, the beautiful, the beautiful river, gather with the saints at the river, that flows by the throne of God."[357]

I heard someone else say:

"In the sweet by and by, we shall meet on that beautiful shore; In the sweet by and by, we shall meet on that beautiful shore."[358]

An acquaintance of mine named Isaiah Martin shared this promise with some of those who were leaving:

"I will meet you in the morning, just inside the Eastern Gate; Then be ready, faithful pilgrim, lest with you it be too late.

If you hasten off to glory, linger near the Eastern Gate; For I'm coming in the morning, so you'll not have long to wait.

Keep your lamps all trimmed and burning, for the Bridegroom watch and wait; He'll be with us at that meeting, just inside the Eastern Gate.

Oh, the joys of that glad meeting, with the saints who for us wait; What a blessed, happy meeting, just inside the Eastern Gate."[359]

Albert Brumley came to say his farewell to several traveling companions. I had heard him tell others,

"If we never meet again this side of Heaven,"[360]

...a reunion was certain to occur in the Shining City. Now it was apparent that the time of the temporary separation had come. To one friend Mr. Brumley said,

"I will meet you in the morning."[361]

...and to another he declared,

"I will meet you by the river."[362]

As he walked away from his friends for the last time on the train, I thought I heard Mr. Brumley whisper:

"Jesus, hold my hand."[363]

I even saw Aunt Fanny there, saying good-bye to the departing passengers. I confess I was somewhat surprised that she was not among those transferring to the special train. Her health appeared to be declining as her body looked very frail. Nevertheless, she joined in the process, sharing final sentiments with several friends who formed a line to tell her good-bye. She too challenged them to meet her in the Shining City:

"On the happy, golden shore, where the faithful part no more, When the storms of life are o'er, Meet me there; Where the night dissolves away into pure and perfect day, I am going home to stay, Meet me there.

Where the harps of angels ring, and the blest forever sing, In the palace of the King, Meet me there; Where in sweet communion we will blend, heart to heart, and friend with friend, in a world that ne'er shall end, Meet me there."[364]

As I beheld this sacred scene, I reflected on what I just experienced. I felt great assurance that many wonderful reunions awaited the saints. It occurred to me that no two followers of The Prince ever say good-bye for the last time. Evidently within the Shining City there are several places where loved ones will see each other once more when their personal journeys are complete.[365] By the river, on the shore, inside the gate, in the morning, by the Life Tree, in the palace of the King… all of these and more will be sites for the saints to encounter one another again in eternity. But which of these is the choice place for such a victorious moment? A passenger named Jeremiah Rankin perhaps said it best as he called out to our friends as they exited the train for their connecting passage to glory:

> *"God be with you till we meet again, by His counsels guide, uphold you, with His sheep securely fold you, God be with you till we meet again.*
>
> *Till we meet, till we meet, Till we meet at Jesus' feet; Till we meet, till we meet, God be with you till we meet again."*[366]

And then I saw him! My heart skipped a beat when I caught sight of my old mentor, Johnson Oatman. I had not seen him for many weeks. He had recently re-connected with our train, but now had received the summons for the faster trip to the Shining City. He appeared weary and worn yet embraced me with a firm handshake and a passionate hug. I whispered some private words of appreciation into his ear, while he spoke his final admonition to me:

> *"If I walk in the pathway of duty, if I work till the close of the day; I shall see the great King in His beauty, when I've gone the last mile of the way.*
>
> *If for Christ I proclaim the glad story, if I seek for His sheep gone astray; I am sure He will show me His glory, when I've gone the last mile of the way.*
>
> *Here the dearest of ties we must sever, tears of sorrow are seen every day; But no sickness, no sighing forever, when I've gone the last mile of the way.*

*And if here I have earnestly striven and have tried all His will to obey;
'twill enhance all the rapture of Heaven, when I've gone the last mile
of the way.*"[367]

How grateful I felt for one more gift of wise counsel from this beloved
friend. He motioned for me to lean closer to him. As I did, he whispered
into my ear:

*"And upon the streets of glory when we reach the other shore and have
safely crossed the Jordan's rolling tide; You will find me shouting 'glory!'
just outside my mansion door, where I'm living on the Hallelujah
Side."*[368]

I remembered and smiled as we parted with a promise to meet again
in the beloved city to come.

Some of our remaining group went to vacant windows in the Coach
Cars and waved final good-byes as a few of the suffering saints turned
around to do the same before they boarded their awaiting ride to the
Shining City. Adger Pace waved from a window next to me and I saw tears
stream down his face as he grasped the promise there would be a:

"Glad reunion day."[369]

A porter confirmed that hopeful cry and reminded all of us that the
reunion would be swift and sure.

Our gathering ended and I prepared to return to my berth in the
Sleeping Car for the night. However, when I went back by the Lounge Car,
I saw that most of those who gathered with us decided to return here as
well. Seeing some of our suffering friends slip on ahead of us caused us
all to reflect on our own home-going time that was coming. Aunt Fanny
was never at a loss for words. She was the first to speak up when we
re-assembled:

*"Someday the silver cord will break, and I no more as now shall sing;
But O the joy when I shall wake, within the palace of the King.*

And I shall see Him face to face – and tell the story saved by grace.[370]

The thought of that coming moment for her caused several people to smile or weep. Another lady who I did not know spoke out and said:

"How beautiful Heaven must be, sweet home of the happy and free; Fair haven of rest for the weary, How beautiful Heaven must be."[371]

Someone asked where the Shining City was and why it seemed so far away. A gentleman named Virgil Brock replied that our blessed destination is not remote at all. As a matter of fact, he claimed it is just:

"Beyond the sunset."[372]

Those who did not know our Prince could never comprehend these happenings. We were all envious of those who received the summons to hasten to the beloved City.

We then began to speculate on what transpires when those on that faster train arrive at the heavenly station. One of the porters reminded us that The Schedule clearly states that "eyes have never seen, nor ears heard, the things that God has prepared for those who love Him."[373] While we knew that truth, we could not help but wonder out loud about what waited so soon for them. Another man, I think someone called him Don, summarized his understanding in two words:

"Finally Home."[374]

Fellow traveler James C. Moore also made a great point. Everyone noticed that almost all of those taken on the rapid train to the Shining City were aged. He expressed that one of the great blessings of that future abode for us all is that we will no longer grow old:

"When our work here is done and our life crown is won, and our troubles and trials are o'er; All our sorrows will end and our voices will blend, with the loved ones who've gone on before.

Never grow old, never grow old, in a land where we'll never grow old;
Never grow old, never grow old, In a land where we'll never grow old."[375]

The thought of such a place seemed almost too glorious to comprehend! No wonder the esteemed apostle had hand-written in The Schedule that "the sufferings of this world were not even worthy to be compared with the glory that would be revealed in us."[376] As sad as these difficult moments were to endure, they could not diminish the coming day of gladness that will never end. We knew that the hour was late, and we needed to dismiss for the night. The porter pointed at two men and instructed them to leave us with a closing thought. Their remarks complemented each other. The first gentleman said:

> "*At the sounding of the trumpet when the saints are gathered home, we will greet each other by the crystal sea; With the friends and all the loved ones there awaiting us to come, What a gathering of the faithful that will be.*"[377]

The second man, Brother Hewitt, had the last word. I had visited with him before and knew that he would have the perfect thoughts for us to hear to end this difficult day. I was not disappointed when he began:

> "*Sing the wondrous love of Jesus, sing His mercy and His grace; In the mansions bright and blessed, He'll prepare for us a place.*
>
> *While we walk the pilgrim pathway, clouds will overspread the skies; But when traveling days are over, not a shadow, not a sigh.*
>
> *Let us then be true and faithful, trusting serving, every day; Just one glimpse of Him in glory, will the toils of life repay.*
>
> *Onward to the prize before us, soon His beauty we'll behold; Soon the pearly gates will open, we shall tread the streets of gold.*"[378]

Thinking about us all being in Heaven together one day provided a perfect way to end our evening. We quickly disbursed and each person went to their own berth. I walked back part of the way with a fine Christian gentleman, Warren Cornell. He had become a good friend since I met him even before going to Calvary. We talked about how the day began with such sorrow but now closed in tender peace. We parted for the night, but only after he left me with this observation:

> "*And I think when I rise to that city of peace, where the Author of peace I shall see; That one strain of the song which the ransomed will sing, in that heavenly kingdom will be.*
>
> '*Peace, peace, wonderful peace, coming down from the Father above, sweep over my spirit forever I pray, in fathomless billows of love.*"[379]

The first time he talked about this divine peace many days ago it seemed like an unattainable dream. Tonight, it lingered as a blessed reality.

Chapter Fifteen –

THE SECOND COMING

The sanctuary filled quickly for the next Lord's Day Chapel. The announced subject "The Second Coming of Christ" piqued the interest of almost every passenger. As always, the porters shared numerous Scriptures to begin the session.[380] After that, Edward Mote stood to address the crowd. I had not seen him since early on my journey when he likened The Prince to "The Solid Rock." This time he set the stage for the discussion at hand:

> *"When He shall come with trumpet sound, O may I then in Him be found; Dressed in His righteousness alone, faultless to stand before the throne."*[381]

A gentleman I did not know, Allan Frazier, also made a few remarks about what will happen:

> *"When Jesus Comes in the Clouds."*[382]

His words also stirred the listeners.

Aunt Fanny followed him. I could scarce imagine having a chapel service without her input. She chose to ask a series of questions for our reflection.

"When Jesus comes to reward His servants, whether it be noon or night; Faithful to Him will He find us watching, with our lamps all trimmed and bright?

Oh, can we say we are ready, brother? Ready for the soul's bright home? Say, will He find you and me still watching, Waiting, waiting when the Lord shall come?"[383]

Many of us on the train showed much interest in *when* The Prince would come back. However, these two speakers reminded us, that readiness for His return remained more important than knowing the specific time of the event. A gentleman seated in the crowd named James Black responded to Aunt Fanny's questions:

"When the trumpet of the Lord shall sound and time shall be no more, and the morning breaks eternal bright and fair; When the saved of earth shall gather over on the other shore, And the roll is called up yonder I'll be there."[384]

Several passengers nodded their heads in agreement and Daniel Warner echoed the same sentiment:

"My name is in the Book of Life, O bless the name of Jesus; I rise above all doubt and strife and read my title clear,

I know, I know my name is there; I know, I know my name is written there."[385]

I recalled reading that The Prince encouraged us to rejoice over that wonderful reality.[386] Our names are written in the Shining City!

After personal preparation for The Prince's return received the primary emphasis, the agenda turned to a theological discussion of what happens when the Church is caught up to meet the Lord. Once again Aunt Fanny provided the clearest articulation of what The Schedule said about that future time:

> "When the trump of the great archangel, its mighty tones shall sound, And the end of the age proclaiming shall pierce the depths profound.
>
> When the Son of Man shall come in His glory to take the saints on high, what a shouting in the skies from the multitudes that rise, Changed in the twinkling of an eye.
>
> When He comes in the clouds descending, and they who loved Him here, from their graves shall awake and praise Him, with joy and not with fear.
>
> When the body and the soul are united, and clothed no more to die, what a shouting there will be when each other's face we see, Changed in the twinkling of an eye."[387]

These words provided much clarity and hope to several passengers who recently said "good-bye" to fellow pilgrims. Some were wondering where their loved ones were at that moment and if they would have a part in the grand event when The Prince returned. A porter explained that at death, the spirit and soul go to be with The Great Conductor, the Father of The Prince, while the body is disposed of somewhere on earth. But at "the rapture" event there will be a resurrection and a reunion of spirit, soul, and body forever and ever.[388] The porter's explanation inspired Aunt Fanny to add:

> "Oh, the seed that was sown in weakness shall then be raised in power, And the songs of the blood bought millions shall hail that blissful hour.
>
> When we gather safely home in the morning, and night's dark shadows fly; What a shouting on the shore when we meet to part no more, Changed in the twinkling of an eye."[389]

Her eloquent description of mortal putting on immortality brought calm assurance and hope to those of us assembled in the chapel. We could not comprehend the train being immediately transported to the final station at the Shining City. No wonder the porters reminded us from The Schedule that this great event is called a "mystery."[390]

Another invited guest achieved great notoriety for his writings about the Lord's return. Brother R.E. Winsett arrived to also address this subject at the chapel service. His comments sounded remarkably like those delivered by Aunt Fanny:

"In the great triumphant morning when we hear The Bridegroom cry, and the dead in Christ shall rise; We'll be changed to life immortal, in the twinkling of an eye.

And meet Jesus in the skies… We shall all rise to meet Him, we shall all go to greet Him, In the morning when the dead in Christ shall rise; We shall all rise to meet Him, we shall all go to greet Him, and shall have the marriage supper in the skies.

In the great triumphant morning when the harvest is complete, and the dead in Christ shall rise; We'll be crowned with life immortal, Christ and all the loved ones meet, In the rapture in the skies."[391]

The rapture. The resurrection of the dead. The completed harvest. The marriage supper. Crowned with immortality. Meeting all our loved ones. Brother Winsett and a porter explained them all. No wonder the guest speaker called it *"The Great Triumphant Morning."* Brother Winsett then excited all the congregants with these stirring words:

"Jesus is coming soon."[392]

Several in the crowd responded with an affirming "amen." One of the porters added that it may be even sooner than soon! Brother Winsett then posed a personal challenge when he asked:

"Will you meet me over yonder?"[393]

His question reminded me of the farewell gathering for some departing saints that we shared not long ago. A woman named Mae Taylor Roberts did not take his question to be rhetorical. She raised her hand, stood on her feet, and spoke for all the assembly:

"There is going to be a meeting in the air, in the sweet, sweet by and by, I am going to meet you, meet you there, in that home beyond the sky; Such singing you will hear, never heard by mortal ear, 'Twill be glorious I do declare, and God's own Son will be the leading One, at the meeting in the air."[394]

These declarations led to someone shouting from the crowd:

"Hallelujah, We Shall Rise."[395]

Brother Winsett then closed out his part of the program with a prayer, which included this request:

"Lift me up above the shadows when to earth You come again,

Let us be in the assembly as Thy Bride to ever reign;

In Thy kingdom full of glory, with our friends we'll ever be,

Lift us up above the shadows there to dwell eternally."[396]

A familiar figure from the back of the room raised his hand and asked if he could say a word. The group whispered to themselves with surprise when they realized it was the converted slave trader, John Newton. He apparently re-joined our journey at one of the many stops along the way. Brother Newton must have been inspired by Aunt Fanny's phrase about meeting "to part no more." A porter reminded us all, that even though The Prince's surprise appearing would happen so quick that it could not be quicker, this event will in fact inaugurate eternity. Mr. Newton added:

"When we've been there ten thousand years bright shining as the sun;

We've no less days to sing God's praise than when we first begun."[397]

What a blessed thought! After ten thousand years in the Shining City, we will have not lost a single day.

Another person I did not know shared how close he believed we were to the return of The Prince. He exclaimed:

"*I can almost hear trumpets!*"[398]

The expressions on the faces of the listeners revealed that they shared the same thrill as the speaker. Before the chapel concluded, the theme shifted to The Prince returning to reign on planet earth. Not only does The Schedule talk about His coming *for* His saints, that holy register also declares He will also come back *with* His saints to rule as King over this planet.[399] Brother James Kirk presented this part of the lesson. His teaching also resonated with this captive audience:

> "*Jesus' coming back will be the answer to earth's sorrowing cry, For the knowledge of the Lord shall fill the earth, the sea, and sky; God will take away all sickness and the sufferer's tears will dry, when our Savior shall come back to earth again.*
>
> *Then the sin and sorrow, pain and death of this dark world shall cease, in a glorious reign with Jesus of a thousand years of peace; All the earth is groaning, crying for that day of sweet release, for our Jesus shall come back to earth again.*
>
> *O our Lord is coming back to earth again, Yes, our Lord is coming back to earth again; Satan will be bound a thousand years, we'll have no tempter then, After Jesus shall come back to earth again.*"[400]

Two things stood out to me from this innovative presentation. First, he said:

> "*All the earth is groaning, crying for that day of sweet release.*"

The porters had pointed this out to us from the Romans part of The Schedule.[401] I immediately thought that this assertion explains the reason for the earthquakes, hurricanes, tornadoes, and floods. We battled some of these catastrophes on this train trip. Second, Brother Kirk declared:

"Satan will be bound a thousand years, we'll have no tempter then."

What a wonderful promise! I could hardly imagine what it would be like to live in a world without the Tempter. Yet on the final pages of The Schedule we are told that the Tempter will be consigned to the bottomless pit for a thousand years and then ultimately in the Lake of Fire forever.[402] (I noticed he appeared to be absent from this present occasion on the train.) The thought of the Tempter being banished made me long for the coming of The Prince of Peace even more.

At this point in the proceedings, a different porter stepped forth with a cablegram from Brother Charles Wesley, which he read to the group:

"Lo, He comes with clouds descending, once for favored sinners slain, Thousand, thousands, saints attending, swell the triumph of His train; Hallelujah! Hallelujah! Hallelujah! God appears on earth to reign,"[403]

Upon hearing the message from Wesley, many in the crowd spoke out loud:

"Hallelujah! Hallelujah! Hallelujah!"

The chapel service ended with three men being invited to the platform. Two of them were familiar to me, but the third one I had not seen before. I smiled to see Stuart Hine and H.G. Spafford once again. This was the third time I had heard them both speak. I recalled that the two of them together had admonished me on the caboose about the cross when I was lost and needed a Savior. Now they were each adding a closing word to the message of the second coming of Jesus, The Crown Prince of Calvary. Stuart Hine spoke first:

"When Christ shall come with shouts of acclamation, and takes me home, what joy shall fill my heart; Then I shall bow in humble adoration, and there proclaim, 'My God, how great Thou art.'"[404]

His words stirred the assembly so much that some hearing him bowed down at their seats and began to magnify The Conductor, the great engineer of salvation. Spafford, the lawyer, spoke next:

"And Lord haste the day when my faith shall resound, the clouds be rolled back like a scroll, The trumpet shall sound, and the Lord shall descend, even so, it is well with my soul."[405]

"It is well,"

...answered the audience. First one and then another, then soon everyone was chanting:

"It is well with my soul."

The final word came from a younger man, Stuart Hamblen. I knew his name sounded familiar, but I could not place him. Suddenly, I remembered he was the man who passed me the note in that chapel service months ago that affirmed the Conductor would do for me, what He had done for other people. Now he left us with a reminder of what the porters taught us – that we should:

"Occupy until He comes."[406]

Passengers waiting for the appearance of The Prince should not just sit idly by staring out at the windows day after day. On the contrary, our best efforts ought to be engaged in the business of His kingdom. Young Hamblen described our assigned activity up until that grand and climactic moment when we will reach the Shining City.

"Until then" he exhorted the audience to continue their worship to and their works for the Conductor.[407]

I got to speak with Aunt Fanny after the chapel session. I thanked her for her contribution to the service. She deflected the complement by saying:

"Praise Him, Praise Him! Jesus, our blessed Redeemer! Heavenly portals loud with hosannas ring; Jesus, Savior, reigneth forever and ever.

Crown Him! Crown Him! Prophet and Priest and King! Christ is coming! Over the world victorious, power and glory unto the Lord belong.

Praise Him! Praise Him! Tell of His excellent greatness; Praise Him! Praise Him! Ever in joyful song."[408]

I commented to her that she always seemed so excited about the return of The Prince. She smiled and left me with one last thought from her for the day:

"When clothed in His brightness, transported I'll rise, to meet Him in clouds of the sky; His perfect salvation, His wonderful love, I'll shout with the millions on high."[409]

Whenever we had an especially blessed chapel, the passengers would discuss it throughout the day and sometimes much longer. So it unfolded on this Lord's Day. I engaged in three separate conversations that greatly enhanced our early morning service.

The first came as I left the Dining Car at the lunch hour. I enjoyed a delicious meal, and fellowship, with some passenger friends. An older gentleman seated at the table nearest the door motioned for me to come over to him. His badge identified him as Carl Blackmore. He too had attended the Second Coming Chapel. He told me that the comeback of The Prince served, indeed, as the blessed hope of his life. He testified with precision:

"Some glorious morning sorrow will cease, some glorious morning all will be peace; Heartaches all ended, school days all done, Heaven will open, Jesus will come."

Some golden daybreak Jesus will come, some golden daybreak battles all won; He'll shout the victory, break through the blue, Some golden daybreak for me, for you."[410]

One phrase from his speech leaped into my spirit: "school days all done." We both vividly recalled our youth when the school day was over. Especially, the last day of school before the summer vacation break. How we would run home as fast as we could to begin this exciting time. Now, this aged follower of The Prince recognized that his education in the life-school of God's grace neared the end. Even though I was much younger than this brother, I too felt the "school days" of life were almost gone and Jesus' coming made me want to run home to meet Him.

I met the second person in the Coach Car that afternoon. I almost drifted to sleep before a younger man asked if he could occupy the seat across from mine. I recognized him as Gordon Jensen. A few weeks earlier he had ministered to me when I walked through a difficult trial. He encouraged me then with the assurance that:

"Tears are a Language God Understands."[411]

Now we talked about many things including today's chapel topic. One of the nagging questions I had concerned the long delay in the return of The Prince. A porter pointed out that the Apostle Peter dealt with that issue in The Schedule.[412] Gordon Jensen added this insight:

"Years of time have come and gone, since I first heard it told, How Jesus would come again some day; If back then it seemed so real, then I just can't help but feel, How much closer His coming is today.

Signs of the times are everywhere, there's a brand new feeling in the air; Keep your eyes upon the eastern sky.

Lift up your head, redemption draweth nigh.

Wars and strife on every hand, and violence fills our land, Still some people doubt that He'll ever come again.

But the Word of God is true, He'll redeem His chosen few, Don't lose hope, soon Christ Jesus will descend."[413]

I realized while listening to his reasoning that every day that passes by does not push us further away from the second coming of The Prince. I sensed that we were closer to the return than ever before.

The last man I spoke with was Daniel Whittle. We met in the Lounge Car in the evening hours and talked until they were just a few minutes away from closing that car for the night. He helped me with one final lingering issue I wrestled with concerning end time events. Why did so many people believe differently about the last days? How could great numbers of saints who loved The Schedule be so wrong and how could we know who truly was right? Daniel Whittle helped me understand that we may not have all the details of The Prince's return figured out, but the important thing is to know The Prince. We may not agree on the *timing* of the second coming, but we can agree on the *fact* of it. Whittle said it this way:

> *"I know not why God's wondrous grace to me He hath made known; Nor why, unworthy, Christ in love, redeemed me for His own.*
>
> *I know not how this saving faith to me He did impart; Nor how believing in His Word, wrought peace within my heart.*
>
> *I know not how the Spirit moves, convincing men of sin; Revealing Jesus through the Word, creating faith in Him.*
>
> *I know not what of good or ill, may be reserved for me; Of weary ways or golden days before His face I see.*
>
> *I know not when my Lord may come, at night or noon-day fair; Nor if I walk the vale with Him, or meet Him in the air.*
>
> *But I know Whom I have believed and am persuaded that He is able; To keep that which I've committed, unto Him against that day."*[414]

Those last sentences he shared found permanent lodging in my mind. We soon parted and I headed for my berth in the Sleeping Car. The final two people I saw that night were a governor and a young fellow with his guitar named Rusty. We passed each other in the corridor just before I reached my resting place. As we brushed by each other, I heard Rusty say:

"I believe He's coming back like He said."[415]

The governor nodded his head and the two of them said together at the same time:

"I wouldn't take nothing for my journey now."[416]

It had been a fulfilling day. As I laid down on my bed, I rehearsed in my mind all that I had heard the past several hours. The governor and the young man had said it best. Every mile of the trip had been worth it, and I was counting on making it to the Shining City. When I finished my evening prayer, I closed my eyes. A few moments later I heard the faint sound of a guitar being played down the corridor at the other end of the Sleeper Car as a robust voice sang:

"I Wouldn't Take Nothing for my Journey Now."[417]

I whispered "Amen," smiled a weary smile, and went to sleep.

Chapter Sixteen –
THE SHINING CITY

Expectancy filled all the passengers. Everyone on board sensed that they were nearing their promised home. Even strangers seemed quick to share that sentiment with each other. For example, one morning I passed one of the frequent chapel speakers, Reverend Cleavant Derricks, in a corridor of the train. We had never met, but I spoke to him and asked, "How are you, Sir?" He smiled and replied:

"We'll soon be done with troubles and trials."[418]

As I walked toward the Dining Car I saw a group of people gathered around someone speaking. My mind flashed back to my first morning on the train when I was on my way to breakfast. That was the first time I heard Aunt Fanny. Sure enough, that scene occurred again. I passed by in time to hear her describe our destination this way:

"There's a city that looks o'er the valley of death, and the glories can never be told; There the sun never sets, and the leaves never fade, in that beautiful city of gold.

There the sun never sets and the leaves never fade; And the eyes of the faithful our Savior behold, in that beautiful city of gold.

There our King, our Redeemer, the Lord whom we love, all the faithful with rapture behold; There the righteous forever shall shine as the stars, in that beautiful city of gold.

Every soul we have led to the foot of the cross, every lamb we have brought to the fold; shall be kept as bright jewels our crown to adorn, in that beautiful city of gold."[419]

Later that day I walked past the corner where Albert Brumley sat. We exchanged greetings and I asked him where he was headed that morning. He replied:

"I'm bound for that city."[420]

I then asked my special friend how far he thought we were from that city and when we would arrive. He pointed me in the direction of James Crutchfield, a passenger I recognized, but had not yet met. He sat in the first seat in the adjoining Coach Car. I went up to him and introduced myself before posing to him the same question. He responded to me:

"Someday beyond the reach of mortal ken, some day God only knows just where and when; The wheels of mortal life shall all stand still, and I shall go to dwell on Zion's Hill."[421]

Yes, only the Conductor knew "just where and when."[422] I took note of his mention of "Zion's Hill." At the last train stop an exuberant delegation came on board, led by Isaac Watts, who had been on the *Ecclesia Express* in the earliest part of my journey. This lively group appeared so passionate as they shouted together in unison:

"Come we that love the Lord and let our joys be known, join in a song with sweet accord, and thus surround the throne.

We're marching to Zion, beautiful, beautiful Zion; We're marching upward to Zion, the beautiful city of God.

Let those refuse to sing, who never knew our God; but children of the heavenly King, may speak their joys abroad.

Then let our songs abound, and every tear be dry; We're marching through Immanuel's ground, to fairer worlds on high."[423]

It seemed like everyone had the Shining City on their lips, their hearts, and their minds. I decided to step out on the caboose for a few minutes that morning. I walked through the last Coach Car connected to it. Along the way I stopped and spoke briefly to a few passengers that I knew on the journey. William Hunter sat in the second seat on the left. I asked him how he was feeling today. He replied:

"My heavenly home is bright and fair, I feel like traveling on; No pain nor death can enter there, I feel like traveling on.

Its glittering towers the sun outshine, I feel like traveling on; That heavenly mansion shall be mine, I feel like traveling on.

Let others seek a home below, I feel like traveling on; Which flames devour or waves o'er flow, I feel like traveling on."[424]

After a short conversation with him I walked a few rows down the center until I saw William Featherston sitting on the right side, reading from his copy of The Schedule. I had heard him in the Communication Car several weeks ago as he expressed his praise to The Prince, saying:

"My Jesus I love Thee, I know Thou art mine, for Thee all the follies of sin I resign; My gracious Redeemer, my Savior art Thou, if ever I loved Thee, my Jesus, 'tis now."[425]

After conversing with him for a few moments I asked him what he looked forward to the most in the future. He answered without hesitation as he spoke of The Prince and pointed above:

"In mansions of glory and endless delight, I'll ever adore Thee in Heaven so bright; I'll sing with the glittering crown on my brow, if ever I loved Thee, my Jesus, 'tis now."[426]

Our dialogue became interrupted by someone two rows behind on the other side, waving for me to come over. Three people were sitting in this compartment. One of them said to me,

"Listen to the dreams they had last night."

(I remember thinking, *this* is a dream. So, this became a 'dream within the dream.') That is, two dreams by two different passengers. An older gentleman named Frederick Weatherly told me about his dream first:

"And once again the scene was changed, New Earth there seemed to be, I saw the Holy City, beside the tideless sea; The light of God was on its streets, the gates were open wide, and all who would, might enter, and no one was denied.

No need of moon or stars by night, or sun to shine by day, It was the New Jerusalem that would not pass away, It was the New Jerusalem that would not pass away...

Jerusalem! Jerusalem! Sing for the night is o'er; Hosanna in the highest! Hosanna forevermore!"[427]

Before I could even comment on his fascinating dream, the lady seated next to him, Nettie Dudley Washington, began to share with me her own dream from last night:

"I dreamed of that city called Glory, so bright and so fair, When I entered the gate I cried 'Holy,' the angels all welcomed me there; They led me from mansion to mansion, and oh, the sights I saw, but I said, 'I want to see Jesus, the One who died for all.'

Then I bowed on my knees and cried 'Holy,' 'Holy,' 'Holy,' I clapped my hands and sang 'Glory,' 'Glory to the Son of God.'

I thought when I entered that city, my loved ones knew me well, they showed me all through Heaven, the scenes are too numerous to tell; I saw Abraham, Isaac, and Jacob, Mark, Luke, and Timothy, But I said, 'I want to see Jesus, the One who died for me.'[428]

These two dreams magnified the excitement I felt concerning the Shining City. I asked them if they would write down some of what they told me so I could contemplate it in more detail. They both agreed. Just before I reached the door to step out on to the caboose, I noticed a young woman sitting on the back row, busy writing feverishly with pen and paper. She looked up at me and smiled. I returned the smile and commented that she seemed excited about her writing. I then remembered that she had spoken in a chapel service about *"Marvelous Grace"*[429] a few weeks earlier. I vividly recalled something she said during that session about The Prince:

"He looked beyond my fault and saw my need."[430]

I asked her why she appeared to be so jubilant. She replied:

"I've never been this homesick before."[431]

I knew she was referring to the Shining City. When I inquired about her joy she responded:

"The holy hills of Heaven call me."[432]

I asked her what made that grand destination so desirable. She responded:

"Tears will never stain the streets of that city."[433]

While I rejoiced at her hopeful statement, she added something even better:

"We shall behold Him."[434]

I agreed with her that seeing The Prince will be the eternal highlight of Heaven.

I asked her what if she died before The Prince came back for us. She readily replied that she did not fear dying because she was living "*Sheltered in the arms of God.*"[435]

I nodded my head and left her to her writing with a blessing as I reached the door of the caboose. When I stepped outside, Nancy Harmon stood on that platform. (Someone always seemed to be there every time I went outside.) The difference today was that Nancy did not face the tracks in the direction we had traveled from, rather she stood sideways and gazed at the sights on one side that we passed. I asked her why she was not looking in the usual way and her response caught me by surprise. She said:

> "*I've come too far to look back, my feet have walked through the valleys, I've climbed mountains, crossed rivers, desert places I've known; But I'm nearing the home shore, the redeemed are rejoicing, Heaven's angels are singing, I've come too far to look back.*"[436]

Her determination inspired me once more. I recall speaking to only one more person that day. Charles Tillman was an older brother in the Faith whose steps were getting unsteady, but his commitment to the Conductor remained resolute. I also asked him how he felt and what he looked forward to the most. He quickly replied:

> "*He loves me too well to forsake me, or give me a trial too much, All His people have been clearly purchased, and Satan can never claim such.*
>
> *By and by I shall see Him and praise Him, in the city of unending day, And the toils of the road will seem nothing, when I get to the end of the way.*
>
> *When the last, feeble step has been taken, and the gates of that city appear, And the beautiful songs of the angels, float out on my listening ear.*
>
> *When all that now seems so mysterious, will be bright and as clear as the day, Then the toils of the road will seem nothing, when I get to the end of the way.*"[437]

I marveled at his attitude and secretly wished for the same in my own heart.

I am not sure I have the language to tell you what happened next. The last few pages of The Schedule became more and more precious to me the further the train rolled down the tracks.[438] The porters and the people greeted one another with "Maranatha" – a constant reminder that the return of The Prince drew near.[439] And then it happened! Not long after that last chapel on "The Second Coming," on an ordinary day that ended with a "y," suddenly the train came to a screeching halt. The Ecclesia Express blew a magnificent whistle – so loud that it sounded like the blast of a trumpet. A mighty messenger from the heavenly realm cried out a shout of welcome. And then we all heard Him for the first time – the voice of The Prince Himself as He called out "COME" as His angelic entourage echoed "for all things are now ready." The porters lifted their voices to tell us what we already knew:

"We are here at last – the last stop, the Shining City."

Every passenger hastened toward the doors, with many stopping to gaze through the windows in hopes of the first look at the land of their dreams. We had heard so much about it, all that remained was for it to come into view and be enjoyed forever. By the time I arrived at the crowded exit, every window was occupied by an eager traveler ready to behold the destination. I thought for a moment they might be most anxious to see the twelve gates of the Shining City, or the river of life that flows from the throne, or the tree of life with its various fruits, or the dwelling places especially prepared for them, or the golden streets or gates of pearl, but no, they were all longing to see the same sight – The Prince! At the first window was a man holding his ticket that bore his name, Rufus Cornelius. I heard him say:

"*Oh I want to see Him, look upon His face, there to sing forever of His saving grace; On the streets of glory, let me lift my voice, Cares all past, home at last, ever to rejoice.*"[440]

At the next window sat a younger woman named Carrie Breck. Her eyes were as big as silver dollars as she exclaimed:

"*Face to face with Christ, my Savior, face to face – what will it be? When with rapture I behold Him, Jesus Christ who died for me?*

Face to face – oh, blissful moment! Face to face – to see and know; Face to face with my Redeemer, Jesus Christ who loves me so."[441]

Her words reminded me of what Aunt Fanny had said when I heard her speak about being "Saved by Grace" in the chapel many miles ago. I looked around for her, but she alluded my sight. Then I spied her out of the corner of my eye. She was small and frail, crouched down behind other excited passengers. I rushed to get close to her, knowing she was just moments away from experiencing the longing of her life. I reached her area just in time to hear her share with someone next to her:

"*Past the gates of that city in my robe so bright and fair, He will lead me where no tears shall ever fall; In the glad song of ages I shall mingle with delight, but I long to see my Savior first of all.*

I shall know Him, I show know Him, and redeemed by His side I shall stand; I shall know Him, I shall know Him, by the prints of the nails in His hands."[442]

When she mentioned the gates, the gentleman on her other side, a Brother Blom, added:

"*He the pearly gates will open, so that I may enter in; For He purchased my redemption and forgave me all my sin.*"[443]

His words in turn excited another passenger who cried out:

"Sweeping through the gates, sweeping through the gates; In the blood of Calvary's Lamb, saved from every stain I am, Hallelujah, I'll go sweeping through the gates."[444]

Indeed, only because The Prince Himself had become one of us, could we ever hope to become one of His.[445] He was willing to die at Calvary so we could live with Him in the Shining City. I saw Lydia Baxter standing just in front of us. I remembered meeting her at the first breakfast on board. She told countless passengers to "take the name of Jesus with them" as they exited the train and now, she herself was moments away from stepping off the train for the last time. She cried aloud:

"O depth of mercy! Can it be? That gate was left ajar for me? For me? For me? Was left ajar for me.

Beyond the river's brink we'll lay, the cross that here is given; And bear the crown of life away and love Him more in Heaven."[446]

I spied Jim Hill trying to peer through another window. He returned my wave and smile. Just yesterday I had shared a meal with him in the Dining Car. He spoke to me then with great assurance about arriving at the Shining City where sorrow, burdens, and pain would all be absent. He joyfully exclaimed:

"What a day that will be."[447]

Yesterday we did not know that tomorrow would be the day. But we did know that one day, some day would come. And now it has!

G.T. "Dad" Speer was among those getting ready to exit the *Ecclesia Express*. He appeared to be among the most visibly happy men at that scene. He loudly cried,

"Heaven's Jubilee!"[448]

By this time, every passenger on board had crowded into the exit area with smiles on their faces, tears of joy in their eyes, and the ticket to the Shining City in their hands. And we must not forget the porters. They were there too! Faithful in service, they were now ready for Heaven's rewards. A holy hush settled over the rejoicing throng. The anticipation multiplied with every split second that passed. Suddenly, young Bill's voice rang out from his window view:

"*The King is coming! The King is coming!*"[449]

Shouts of euphoria spontaneously burst forth from the redeemed ones on board. Then I heard one final voice from my fellow passengers. It belonged to a gentleman named Edward Perronet. I remembered he traveled with Charles Wesley when he had joined us for part of the journey on the train. I did not recall him saying anything earlier, but I will never forget what he uttered now:

"*All hail the power of Jesus' name, let angels prostrate fall; Bring forth the royal diadem and crown Him Lord of all.*

O that with yonder sacred throng, we at His feet may fall; We'll join the everlasting song and crown Him Lord of all."[450]

Every eye was on the door as immortality began to adorn us. It was at that moment – at that very moment – that the train doors began to open, and I woke up.

"Noooooo…"

I cried out, shaking as I returned to an awakened consciousness. I tried to lay my head back down and close my eyes, but alas, sleep had taken flight from me once again. I called out to my wife who came running into our bedroom. I embraced her with an extended hug and a tender exchange of love for our family. With fevered excitement I told her everything that I just told you, however, I confess I only remembered about half of it.[451] (If the half that has not been told is anything like the half that has, I cannot wait to experience it for the first time.) We rejoiced that reality surely is greater than the dream because I could now make the journey with her and our children together.

When I finally somewhat settled down, my wife went into the kitchen to finish preparing something for us to eat. I walked into my study and closed the door. I saw the picture of my beloved mother and father, and I thanked the Lord for blessing me with someone who raised me on the right train. I thought of all the pastors and teachers who had functioned like the porters in caring for my soul and sharing the Word of God with me. I picked up my Bible and gave special thanks for The Schedule that I could follow to pattern my life after. I took a hymnal from my shelf and as I thumbed through it, I smiled and expressed gratitude for all the fellow passengers that had accompanied me on my own personal journey. I touched the globe on my desk and spun it around, giving thanks for having a part in helping to fulfill the Great Commission.

Finally, I praised My Companion, the Comforter, Advocate, Helper, who has been with me, within me, upon me, and before me every step of the way. I then praised the Conductor, the great Engineer of Salvation, who laid the tracks and sent His only Son, and now is at the wheel bringing all things to their completion. And then I praised The Crown Prince of Calvary, the victor over sin, death, hell, and the grave, who loved me and gave Himself for me, the only worthy one who will reign forever and ever. I wiped my eyes, flooded with tears, and arose to join my wife in the other room. As I left my study and walked toward the dining room I began to softly sing:

> "*The Lord has been so good to me, I feel like traveling on; Until that blessed home I see, I feel like traveling on.*"[452]

ENDNOTES

THE AUTHOR'S EXPLANATION ENDNOTES

1 Singleton, James. "I Will Not Be a Stranger" *Stamps Quartet Music*, 1956

CHAPTER ONE ENDNOTES

2 Revelation 21:23

3 Job 3:17

4 Hebrews 1:1-2

5 John 3:16

6 2 Corinthians 8:9

7 John 16:13-15

8 1 Peter 5:8; 2 Corinthians 11:14

9 Widemeyer, C.B. "Come and Dine" *The Gospel Hymnal* 1973, p. 276

10 Hoffman, Elisha. "Leaning on the Everlasting Arms" *Church Hymnal* 1951, p. 359

11 Stone, Samuel. "The Church's One Foundation" *Hymns for the Family of God* 1976, p. 547

12 Hudson, Ralph. "A Glorious Church" *Worship His Majesty* 1987, p. 350

13 Longstaff, William. "Take Time to Be Holy" *Hymns for the Family of God* 1976, p. 457

14 Ferguson, Manie. "Blessed Quietness" *Hymns for the Family of God* 1976, p. 145

15 Isaiah 57:20-21

16 *Ecclesia* is the Greek word for "church."

17 Cooper, W. Oliver and Dalton, Marvin. "Looking for a City" *Church Hymnal* 1951, pp. 18-19

18 Hebrews 11:10; John 14:3

19 Bliss, Philip P. "Wonderful Words of Life" *Worship His Majesty* 1987, p. 315

20 Carter, Ruth Kelso. "Standing on the Promises" *Church Hymnal* 1951, p. 329

21 Keith, George. "How Firm a Foundation" *Church Hymnal* 1951, p.127

22 Buell, Hattie. "A Child of the King" *Church Hymnal* 1951, 348

23 Watts, Isaac. "Jesus Shall Reign Where'er the Sun" *Hymns for the Family of God* 1976, p. 238

24 Babcock, Maltbie. "This is My Father's World" *Worship His Majesty* 1987, p. 73

25 Stuart Hine. "How Great Thou Art" *Worship His Majesty* 1987, p. 111

26 F.M. Lehman. "The Love of God" *Church Hymnal* 1951, p. 220

27 Ibid.

28 Ellis, V.B. (Vep) "The Love of God" *The Gospel Hymnal* 1973, p. 377

29 Ellis, V.B. (Vep) "I'm in a New World" *Church Hymnal* 1951, p. 94

30 Ellis, V.B. (Vep) "I Have Somebody with Me" *Church Hymnal* 1951, p. 313

31 Ellis, V.B. (Vep) "Have Faith in God" *Church Hymnal* 1951, p. 54

CHAPTER TWO ENDNOTES

32 https://www.christianitytoday.com/history/people/poets/fanny-crosby.html

33 Crosby, Fanny J. "Tell Me the Story of Jesus" *Hymns for the Family of God* 1976, p. 215

34 Ibid.

35 Hankey, Katherine. "I Love to Tell the Story" *Hymns for the Family of God* 1976, p. 619

36 Rowley, Francis. "I Will Sing the Wondrous Story" *Hymns for the Family of God* 1976, p. 618

37 Chapman, J. Wilbur. "One Day" *Hymns for the Family of God* 1976, p. 22

38 Chapman, J. Wilbur. "Jesus! What a Friend for Sinners" *Hymns for the Family of God* 1976, p. 244

39 Ovens, W.G. "Wounded for Me" *Hymns for the Family of God* 1976, p. 282

40 Duffield, George. "Stand Up for Jesus" *Church Hymnal* 1951, p. 381

41 Warner, Anna. "Jesus Loves Me" *Church Hymnal* 1951, p. 87

42 (Unknown). "Jesus Loves the Little Children" *Hymns for the Family of God* 1976, p. 15

43 Gabriel, Charles. "I Stand Amazed" *Hymns for the Family of God* 1976, p. 223

44 Romans 5:6-8

45 Whitfield, Frederick. "O How I Love Jesus" *Hymns for the Family of God* 1976, p. 634

46 Thompson, Will. "Jesus is All the World to Me" *Hymns for the Family of God* 1976, p. 627

47 Long, Lela. "Jesus is the Sweetest Name I Know" *Worship His Majesty* 1987, p. 172

48 Weigle, C.F. "No One Ever Cared for Me Like Jesus" *Worship His Majesty* 1987, p. 648

49 Weigle, C.F. "I Love to Walk with Jesus" Church Hymnal 1951, p. 186

50 Baxter, Lydia. "Take the Name of Jesus with You" *Church Hymnal* 1951, p. 376

51 Song of Solomon 2:1

52 Fry, Charles W. "The Lily of the Valley" *Great Hymns of the Faith* 1968, p. 447

53 Gilmour, Henry. "The Haven of Rest" *Church Hymnal* 1951, pp. 344-345

54 Jones, L.E. "I've Anchored in Jesus" *Church Hymnal* 1951, p. 275

55 Toplady, A.M. "Rock of Ages" *Church Hymnal* 1951, p. 83

56 Mote, Edward. "The Solid Rock" *Worship His Majesty* 1987, p. 443

57 Bliss, Philip P. "I Will Sing of My Redeemer" *Worship His Majesty* 1987, pp. 179-180

58 Bliss, Philip P. "Jesus Loves Even Me" *Worship His Majesty* 1987, p. 456

59 Bliss, Philip P. "Hallelujah, What a Savior!" *Worship His Majesty* 1987, p. 208

60 Dalton, Marvin P. "What a Savior" *The Gospel Hymnal* 1973, p. 260

CHAPTER THREE ENDNOTES

61 Crosby, Fanny J. "Blessed Assurance" *Church Hymnal,* 1951, p. 181

62 Rowe, James. "Love Lifted Me" *Church Hymnal,* 1951, p. 265

63 Warren, B.E. "Joy Unspeakable" *Church Hymnal* 1951, p. 167

64 1 Peter 1:8

65 Cornell, Warren. "Wonderful Peace" *Church Hymnal* 1951, p. 290

66 Warren, B.E. "Victory" *Melodies of Praise* 1957, p. 252

67 Wells, James. "Living by Faith" *Church Hymnal* 1951, p. 162

68 Rinkart, Martin. "Now Thank We All Our God" *Worship His Majesty* 1987, p. 333

69 Grant, Robert. "O Worship the King" *Worship His Majesty* 1987, p. 14

70 Van Dyke, Henry. "Joyful, Joyful We Adore Thee" *Worship His Majesty* 1987, p. 36

71 Watts, Isaac. "I Sing the Mighty Power of God" *The Hymnal for Worship & Celebration* 2019, p. 59

72 Pierpoint, Folliott. "For the Beauty of the Earth" *Worship His Majesty* 1987, p. 76

73 Robinson, Robert. "Come, Thou Fount of Every Blessing" *Worship His Majesty* 1987, p. 30

74 Ken, Thomas. "Doxology" *Hymns for the Family of God* 1976, p. 384

75 Psalm 100:4

76 Matthew 6:9-13

77 Crosby, Fanny J. "Redeemed" *Hymns for the Family of God* 1976, p. 646

78 Crosby, Fanny J. "Praise Him, Praise Him" *Worship His Majesty* 1987, p. 43

79 Crosby, Fanny J. "He Hideth My Soul" *Worship His Majesty* 1987, p. 428

80 Crosby, Fanny J. "To God be the Glory" *Worship His Majesty* 1987, p. 31

81 Wesley, Charles. "Jesus, Lover of My Soul" *Worship His Majesty* 1987, p. 206

82 Wesley, Charles. "Love Divine, All Loves Excelling" *Worship His Majesty* 1987, p. 94

83 Wesley, Charles "And Can it Be That I Should Gain?" *Worship His Majesty* 1987, p. 245

84 Wesley, Charles. "O For a Thousand Tongues to Sing" *Worship His Majesty* 1987, p. 46

85 Heber, Reginald. "Holy, Holy, Holy" *Worship His Majesty* 1987, p. 47

86 Chisholm, Thomas. "Great is Thy Faithfulness" *Hymns for the Family of God* 1976, p. 98

87 Matthew Bridges. "Crown Him with Many Crowns" *Hymns for the Family of God* 1976, p. 345

88 Lillenas, Haldor. "My Wonderful Lord" *Hymns for the Family of God* 1976, p. 368

89 Lillenas, Haldor. "Don't Turn Him Away" *Church Hymnal* 1951, p. 326

CHAPTER FOUR ENDNOTES

90 Hanby, Benjamin. "Who is He in Yonder Stall?" *The Hymnal for Worship & Celebration* 2019, p. 168

91 Watts, Isaac. "Joy to the World" *Worship His Majesty* 1987, p. 135

92 Wesley, Charles. "Come, Thou Long-Expected Jesus" *Worship His Majesty* 1987, p. 121

93 Wesley, Charles. "Hark! the Herald Angels Sing" *Worship His* Majesty 1987, p. 137

94 Longfellow, Henry. "I Heard the Bells on Christmas Day" *Worship His Majesty* 1987, p. 123

95 Crosby, Fanny J. "Saved by Grace" *Worship His Majesty* 1987, p. 685

96 Doddridge, Philip. "Grace 'Tis a Charming Sound" *Hymnary.org* https://hymnary.org/text/grace_tis_a_charming_sound,

97 Luke 8:1-3; John 4:7-29; Mark 5:1-20; Luke 23:32-43

98 Lillenas, Haldor. "Wonderful Grace of Jesus" *Worship His Majesty* 1987, p. 102

99 Luke 18:10-14

100 Newton, John. "Amazing Grace" *Worship His Majesty* 1987, p. 429

101 Ibid.

102 Romans 5:20

103 Johnston, Julia. "Grace Greater Than Our Sin" *Worship His Majesty* 1987, p. 105

104 Ibid.

105 1 John 2:28

106 Wesley, Charles. "Depth of Mercy! Can There Be" *The Broadman Hymnal* 1940, p. 288

107 Excell, E.O. "Grace Enough for Me" *Hymnary.org* https://hymnary. org/text/in_looking_through_my_tears_one_day

CHAPTER FIVE ENDNOTES

108 Matthew 5:45

109 Acts 5:41; Philippians 3:10; 1 Peter 4:12-16; Revelation 2:10

110 Graeff, Frank. "Does Jesus Care?" *Hymns for the Family of God* 1976, p. 517

111 Ibid.

112 Crosby, Fanny J. "All the Way My Savior Leads Me" *Worship His Majesty* 1987, p. 420

113 Genesis 18:25

114 Suffield, Kittie. "God is Still on the Throne" *library.timelesstruths. org* https://library.timelesstruths.org/music/God_Is_Still_on_the_ Throne/

115 Anonymous. "Never Alone" *Church Hymnal* 1951, p. 288

116 Martin, William C. "My Father Watches Over Me" *library.time-lesstruths.org* https://library.timelesstruths.org/music/My_Father_ Watches_Over_Me/

117 Martin, W.C. "Still Sweeter Every Day" *The Gospel Hymnal* 1973, p. 81

118 Martin, Civilla. "His Eye is on the Sparrow" *Worship His Majesty* 1987, p. 354

119 Martin, Civilla. "God Will Take Care of You." *Worship His Majesty* 1987, p. 368

120 Moore, Thomas. "Come, Ye Disconsolate" *The Hymnal for Worship and Celebration* 2019, p. 416

121 Sammis, J.J. "Trust and Obey" *Church Hymnal* 1951, p. 157

122 Stead, Louisa. "Tis So Sweet to Trust in Jesus" *Church Hymnal* 1951, p. 137

123 Gilmore, Joseph. "He Leadeth Me" *Church Hymnal* 1951, p. 335

124 Young, George A. "God Leads us Along" *Church Hymnal* 1951, pp. 364-365

125 Hebrews 11:33-40

126 Acts 12:1-9

127 Stanphill, Ira. "I Know Who Holds Tomorrow" *The Gospel Hymnal* 1973, p. 373

128 Alt, Florence M. "My Life is But a Weaving" *library.timelesstruths.org* https://library.timelesstruths.org/music/My_Life_Is_but_a_Weaving/

129 Spafford, Horatio. "It is Well with My Soul" *Hymns for the Family of God* 1976, p. 495

130 Bridgers, Luther. "He Keeps Me Singing" *Church Hymnal* 1951, p. 125

131 Dorsey, Thomas. "Take My Hand, Precious Lord" *Church Hymnal* 1951, pp. 396-397

132 Acts 9:16

133 2 Corinthians 12:9

134 Flint, Annie Johnson. "He Giveth More Grace" *Hymns for the Family of God,* 1976, p. 112

135 Newton, John. "Amazing Grace" *Church Hymnal* 1951, p. 57

136 Stevens, W.B. "Farther Along" *Church Hymnal* 1951

137 Tindley, Charles. "We'll Understand it Better By and By" *Worship His Majesty,* 1987, p. 701

CHAPTER SIX ENDNOTES

138 Bowring, John. "In the Cross of Christ I Glory" *Worship His Majesty* 1987, p. 229

139 Watts, Isaac. "When I Survey the Wondrous Cross" *Worship His Majesty* 1987, p. 225

140 Bennard, George. "The Old Rugged Cross" *Worship His Majesty* 1987, p. 228

141 Watts, Isaac. "Am I a Soldier of the Cross" *Worship His Majesty* 1987, p. 537

142 Moody, Charles. "Kneel at the Cross" *Church Hymnal* 1951, p. 165

143 Ogden, William. "Look and Live" *Hymns of Glorious Praise* 1969, p. 186

144 John 12:32-33

145 Pounds, Jessie. "The Way of the Cross Leads Home" *Worship His Majesty* 1987, p. 490

146 Henderson, S.J. "Saved by the Blood" *Hymns of Glorious Praise* 1969, p. 203

147 Cowper, William. "There is a Fountain" *Church Hymnal* 1951, p. 379

148 Luke 23:42-43

149 Taylor, Mrs. Walter. "Calvary Covers it All" *Hymns for the Family of God* 1976, p. 250

150 Christiansen, Ava. "Blessed Redeemer" *Hymns for the Family of God* 1976, p. 275

151 Newell, William. "At Calvary" *Hymns for the Family of God* 1976, p. 415

152 Watts, Isaac. "At the Cross" *Hymns for the Family of God* 1976, p. 95

153 Hebrews 12:1

154 Moore, John. "Burdens are Lifted at Calvary" *Hymns for the Family of God* 1976, p. 60

155 Romans 7:15-20

156 Stanphill, Ira. "There's Room at the Cross" *Hymns for the Family of God* 1976, p. 645

CHAPTER SEVEN ENDNOTES

157 Lowry, Robert. "Nothing But the Blood" *Church Hymnal* 1951, pp. 368-369

158 Hoffman, Elisha. "Are You Washed in the Blood" *Church Hymnal* 1951, p. 177

159 Jones, L.E. "There is Power in the Blood" *Church Hymnal* 1951, p. 390

160 Waterman, Mrs. Anna. "Yes, I Know" *Melodies of Praise* 1957, p. 230

161 Ibid.

162 Bartlett, E.M. "Victory in Jesus" *Church Hymnal* 1951, p. 120

163 Bartlett, E.M. "Everybody Will be Happy Over There" *Church Hymnal* 1951, p. 180

164 Crouch, Andrae. "The Blood Will Never Lose Its Power" *The Hymnal for Worship & Celebration* 2019, p. 192

165 Hine, Stuart. "How Great Thou Art" *Worship His Majesty* 1987, p. 111

166 Spafford, Horatio. "It is Well with My Soul" *Worship His Majesty* 1987, p. 524

167 Luke 24:21, 26; 1 Corinthians 15:4

168 Pott, Francis. (trans.) "The Strife is O'er *Great Hymns of the Faith* 1968, p. 133

169 Lowry, Robert. "Christ Arose" *Worship His Majesty* 1987, p. 256

170 Ibid.

171 Wesley, Charles. "Christ the Lord is Risen Today" *Worship His Majesty* 1987, p. 259

172 1 Corinthians 15

173 John 20:11-18

174 Miles, C. Austin. "In the Garden" *Hymns for the Family of God* 1976, p. 588

175 Ackley, Alfred. "He Lives!" *Worship His Majesty* 1987, p. 264

176 John 20:27, 28

177 John 20:8

178 Gaither, William J. and Gloria. "Because He Lives" *Worship His Majesty* 1987, p. 260

179 Smith, Oswald. "When Jesus Comes" https://www.hymnal.net/en/hymn/h/1078

CHAPTER EIGHT ENDNOTES

180 Matthew 7:13-14

181 Owens, Priscilla. "Jesus Saves" *Church Hymnal* 1951, p. 97

182 Morris, Lelia. "Stranger of Galilee" *library.timelesstruths.org* https://library.timelesstruths.org/music/The_Stranger_of_Galilee/

183 Hamblen, Stuart. "It is No Secret" *Hymns for the Family of God* 1976, p. 581

184 Storey, Anna. "Looking for Me" *library.timelesstruths.org https://library.timelesstruths.org/music/Looking_for_Me/*

185 Wright, G.E. "When He Reached Down His Hand for Me" *Melodies of Praise* 1957, p. 238

186 Luke 15:4-10

187 Carmichael, Ralph. "The Savior is Waiting" *Hymns for the Family of God* 1976, p. 435

188 Slade, M.B.C. "Who at My Door is Standing?" *The Gospel Hymnal* 1973, p. 309

189 Morris, Lelia. "Let Jesus Come into Your Heart" *Hymns for the Family of God* 1976, p. 433

190 Hart, Joseph. "Come, Ye Sinners, Poor and Needy" *Heart Warming Songs – Number 4* 1970, p. 90

191 Crosby, Fanny J. "Pass Me Not, O Gentle Savior" *Hymns for the Family of God* 1976, p. 416

192 Mark 6:48

193 Thompson, Will. "Softly and Tenderly" *Church Hymnal* 1951, p. 385

194 Kirkpatrick, William. "Lord, I'm Coming Home" *Church Hymnal* 1951, p. 153

195 Luke 15:11-24

196 Luke 9:57-62

197 Bliss, P.P. "Once for All" *The Broadman Hymnal* 1940, p. 340

198 Bliss, Philip P. "Almost Persuaded" *Church Hymnal* 1951, pp. 392-393

199 Acts 26:28-29

200 Mark 12:34

201 Shadduck, Bert. "The Great Judgment Morning" *Church Hymnal* 1951, p. 208

202 Jude 22, 23

203 Reed, Elizabeth. "O Why Not Tonight?" *The Broadman Hymnal* 1940, p. 465

204 2 Corinthians 6:2

205 Elliott, Charlotte. "Just as I Am" *Worship His Majesty* 1987, p. 497

206 Philippians 3:8

207 Clephane, Elizabeth C. "The Ninety and Nine" *The Gospel Hymnal* 1973, p. 337

208 Luke 15:3-7

209 1 Peter 1:18-19

210 Miller, Rhea. "I'd Rather Have Jesus" *Hymns for the Family of God* 1976, p. 650

211 Hebrews 11:24-26

CHAPTER NINE ENDNOTES

212 Gaither, William J. "I've Been to Calvary" *The American Country Hymn Book,* 1975, p. 116

213 Rowe, James. "Redeemed" *Church Hymnal*, 1951, p. 277

214 McDaniel, Rufus. "Since Jesus Came into My Heart" *Church Hymnal* 1951, p. 269

215 Vandall, N.B. "My Sins are Gone" *Church Hymnal* 1951, p. 318

216 Luke 15

217 Luke 15:7, 10

218 Miles, C. Austin. "A New Name in Glory" *Church Hymnal* 1951, p. 154

219 Hoffman, Elisha. "It is Mine" *Hymns of Glorious Praise* 1968, p. 458

220 Sullivan, James P. "Oh! Say, But I'm Glad" *Melodies of Praise* 1957, p. 54

221 Gabriel, Charles. "He Lifted Me" *Worship His Majesty* 1987, p. 629

222 Williams, Clara. "Satisfied" *Worship His Majesty* 1987, p. 444

223 Scholfield, Jack. "Saved, Saved!" *Worship His Majesty* 1987, p. 422

224 Isaiah 45:22; Hebrews 7:25

225 Hoffman, Elisha. "Glory to His Name" *Church Hymnal* 1951, p. 113

226 Ibid.

227 Doddridge, Philip. "O Happy Day!" *Worship His Majesty* 1987, p. 647

228 Morris,Lelia. "What a Savior is Mine" *hymnary*.org https://hymnary.org/text/bethlehem_calvary_olivet_tell

229 Peterson, John. "Heaven Came Down and Glory Filled My Soul" *Worship His Majesty* 1987, p. 630

230 Blandly, E.W. "Where He Leads Me" *Church Hymnal* 1951, p. 65

231 Harris, Margaret. "I Will Praise Him" *Hymns for the Family of God* 1976, p. 359

232 Ibid.

233 Clayton, Norman. "Now I Belong to Jesus" *Hymns for the Family of God* 1976, p. 637

CHAPTER TEN ENDNOTES

234 John 3:3, 7

235 Netherlands Folk Song. "We Gather Together" *Hymns for the Family of God* 1976, p. 387

236 Matthew 26:26-29; Mark 14:22-25; Luke 22:17-20; 1 Corinthians 11:23-26

237 Lemons, M.S. "Remember" *Church Hymnal* 1951, p. 274

238 Hall, Mrs. Elvina. "Jesus Paid it All" *Church Hymnal* 1951, p. 119

239 Pace, Adger. "He's My King" *Church Hymnal* 1951, p. 20

240 Pace, Adger. "Jesus is the One" *Church Hymnal* 1951, p. 273

241 Pace, Adger. "Victory Today is Mine" *Church Hymnal* 1951, p. 239

242 Pace, Adger. "I Can Tell You the Time" *Church* Hymnal 1951, p. 33

243 Graham, F.M. "An Old Account Settled" *Church Hymnal* 1951, p. 176

244 Speer, G.T. "The Dearest Friend I Ever Had" *Church Hymnal* 1951, p. 150

245 Speer, G.T. "I Never Shall Forget the Day" Church Hymnal 1951, p. 130

246 Steele, Mrs. Minnie A. "My Burdens Rolled Away" *The Gospel Hymnal* 1973, p. 280

247 Hussey, Jennie. "Lead Me to Calvary" *Worship His Majesty* 1987, p. 235

248 Crosby, Fanny J. "Near the Cross" *Church Hymnal* 1951, p. 410

249 1 Corinthians 11:26

250 Winsett, R.E. "The Message of His Coming" *Melodies of Praise* 1957, p. 228

251 Vaughan, J.B. "We Shall See the King" *Church Hymnal* 1951, p. 300

252 Proverbs 18:24

253 John 15:15

254 Oatman, Johnson. "I'll Be a Friend to Jesus" *Church Hymnal* 1951, p. 386

255 Oatman, Johnson. "No, Not One" *Church Hymnal,* 1951, 365

256 Oatman, Johnson. "Count Your Blessings" *Worship His Majesty* 1987, p. 82

257 Ibid.

258 Oatman, Johnson. "The Hallelujah Side" *Church Hymnal"* 1951, p. 237

259 Ibid.

260 Oatman, Johnson. "Higher Ground" *Hymns for the Family of God* 1976, p. 469

261 Oatman, Johnson. "When the Redeemed are Gathering In" *Church Hymnal* 1951, p. 319

262 Oatman, Johnson. "I Will Trade the Old Cross for a Crown" *Church Hymnal* 1951, p. 247

CHAPTER ELEVEN ENDNOTES

263 Longstaff, William. "Take Time to be Holy" *Worship His Majesty* 1987, p. 457

264 Ibid.

265 Matt. 5:8; Mark 8:34; John 17:17; Rom. 12:1; 1 Cor. 6:19-20; 2 Cor. 6:14-7:1; Gal. 2:20; Eph. 5:25-27; Phil. 4:8; 1 Thess. 4:3, 7; Titus 2:11-14; Heb. 12:14; 13:12; 1 John 1:7-9; 3:1-3; Rev. 22:11

266 Morris, Mrs. C.H. "Holiness Unto the Lord" *The Gospel Hymnal* 1973, p. 47

267 Arr. By Bill Gaither and Geron Davis. "Highway to Heaven" Gaither Music Company, 2000

268 Nusbaum, Cyrus. "His Way With Thee" *Church Hymnal* 1951, p. 216

269 Pollard, Adelaide. "Have Thine Own Way, Lord" *Hymns for the Family of God* 1976, p. 400

270 Grose, Howard. "Give of Your Best to the Master" *Hymns for the Family of God* 1976, p. 516

271 Brumley, Albert E. "I've Never Been Sorry" *Church Hymnal* 1951, p. 114

272 Brumley, Albert E. "It's a Grand and Glorious Feeling" *Church Hymnal* 1951, p. 28

273 Gaither, William J. "The Longer I Serve Him" *Worship His Majesty* 1987, p. 657

274 Luke 17:32; 1 Timothy 4:10

275 Crosby, Fanny J. "I am Thine, O Lord" *Worship His Majesty* 1987, p.383

276 Havergal, Frances. "Take My Life and Let it Be Consecrated" *Worship His Majesty* 1987, p. 380

277 Romans 6:13-19; 12:1-2; 1 Corinthians 6:19-20; 2 Timothy 2:20-21

278 Adams, Sarah. "Nearer, My God to Thee" *Worship His Majesty* 1987, p. 546

279 Orr, Edwin. "Cleanse Me" *Church Hymnal* 1951, p. 141

280 Psalm 139:23-24

281 Van De Venter, J.W. "I Surrender All" *Church Hymnal* 1951, pp. 354-355

282 Tindley, C.A. "Nothing Between" *Church Hymnal* 1951, p. 395

283 Unknown. "Just a Closer Walk with Thee" *Hymns for the Family of God* 1976, p. 591

284 Jones, Charles Price. "Deeper, Deeper" *Church Hymnal* 1951, p. 230

285 Longstaff, William. "Take Time to be Holy" *Worship His Majesty* 1987, p. 457

286 Psalm 17:15; Song of Solomon 6:3; 1 John 3:2-3

287 Simpson, Albert B. "Himself" *library.timelesstruths.org* https://library. timelesstruths.org/music/Himself/

288 Hewitt, E.E. "More About Jesus" *Church Hymnal* 1951, p. 103

289 Abernathy, Lee Roy. "I Want to Know More About My Lord" *Church Hymnal* 1951, p. 6

290 Battersby, C. Maud. "An Evening Prayer" *hymnary.org* https://hymnary.org/text/if_i_have_wounded_any_soul_today

CHAPTER TWELVE ENDNOTES

291 2 Corinthians 3:18

292 Cousin, Anne Ross. "The Sands of Time are Sinking" *Great Hymns of the Faith* 1968, p. 509

293 Anon. "Is Not This the Land of Beulah?" *The Broadman Hymnal* 1940, p. 27

294 Miles, Austin. "Dwelling in Beulah Land" *Worship His Majesty* 1987, p. 549

295 Numbers 13:27-29; Joshua 14:12

296 Oatman, Miriam. "The Son Hath Made Me Free" *Church Hymnal* 1951, pp. 158-159

297 French, J.E. "This is Like Heaven to Me" *Church Hymnal* 1951, p. 334

298 2 Peter 3:18

299 Rankin, J.E. "Tell it to Jesus Alone" *Church Hymnal* 1951, p. 129

300 Matthew 6:8

301 Hoffman, Elisha. "I Must Tell Jesus" *Church Hymnal* 1951, p. 107

302 Scriven, Joseph. "What a Friend We Have" *Church Hymnal* 1951, p. 341

303 Hawks, Mrs. Annie. "I Need Thee Every Hour" *Church Hymnal* 1951, pp. 330-331

304 Palmer, Ray. "My Faith Looks Up to Thee" *Church Hymnal* 1951, p. 69

305 Walford, W.W. "Sweet Hour of Prayer" *Church Hymnal* 1951, p. 71

306 Ibid.

307 Deuteronomy 34:1-4

308 Tindley, C.A. "Stand by Me" *Church Hymnal* 1951, p. 149

309 1 Peter 5:7

310 Tindley, C. Albert. "Leave it There" *Church Hymnal* p. 164

311 Ellis, Vep. "Let Me Touch Him" *Great Gospel Songs and Hymns* 1976, p. 96

312 Ellis, V.B. (Vep). "I Know He Heard My Prayer" *Church Hymnal* 1951, pp. 16-17

CHAPTER THIRTEEN ENDNOTES

313 Matthew 16:13-16; 22:36-40; 28:18-20

314 Suffield, Mrs. F.W. "Little is Much, When God is in It" *Hymns for the Family of God* 1976, p. 512

315 Crosby, Fanny J. "Rescue the Perishing" *Church Hymnal* 1951, p. 145

316 Thomas, Alexcenah. "Bring Them In" *Church Hymnal* 1951, p. 85

317 Shaw, Knowles. "Bringing in the Sheaves" *Church Hymnal* 1951, p. 109

318 Psalm 126:5-6

319 Mark 6:7; Luke 10:1

320 Luther, C.C. "Must I Go, and Empty-Handed?" *The Broadman Hymnal* 1940, p. 296

321 1 Corinthians 9:22

322 Brown, Mary. "I'll Go Where You Want Me to Go" *Hymns for the Family of God* 1976, p. 502

323 Miles, Charles A. "If Jesus Goes With Me I'll Go" https://library.time-lesstruths.org/music/If_Jesus_Goes_with_Me/

324 Matthew 11:28; John 7:37; Mark 16:15

325 Harmon, Nancy. "I'll Go" *Keep on Singing* 1979, pp. 22-23

326 Romans 3:10, 23; 6:23; 5:8; 10:9, 13

327 Ogden, William. "He is Able to Deliver Thee" *Hymns of Glorious Praise* 1969, p. 182

328 Acts 4:20

329 Brumley, Albert E. "He Set Me Free" *Church Hymnal* 1951, p. 235

330 Zelley, H.J. "He Brought Me Out" *The Gospel Hymnal* 1973, p. 159

331 Acts 8:4; 17:6

332 Acts 1:8

333 Acts 4:31

334 Mackay, William P. "Revive Us Again" *Church Hymnal* 1951, p. 370

335 Tillman, Charlie "The Old Time Power" *Church Hymnal* 1951, p. 121

336 Bottome, Rev. F. "The Comforter has Come" *Church Hymnal* 1951, p. 406

337 Buffum, Herbert. "He Abides" *Church Hymnal* 1951, p. 184

338 John 14:16

339 Gabriel, Charles. "Send the Light" *Church Hymnal* 1951, p. 281

340 2 Corinthians 9:6-7

341 Munsey, Ruth. "An Unfinished Task" *Hemphill Music Company*, 1970

342 Campbell, Lucy E. "He'll Understand and Say Well Done" *Church Hymnal* 1951, p.282

CHAPTER FOURTEEN ENDNOTES

343 Psalm 116:15; Philippians 1:21; 2 Timothy 2:12; Revelation 14:13

344 Fawcett, John "Blest Be the Tie That Binds" *Worship His Majesty* 1987, p. 337

345 Lyte, Henry F. "Abide with Me" *Worship His Majesty* 1987, p. 528

346 Buffum, Herbert. "When I Make My Last Move" *Church Hymnal* 1951, p. 295

347 Buffum, Herbert. "In the City Where the Lamb is the Light" *Songs We Love* 1969, p. 188

348 DeMarbelle, Dion. "When They Ring the Golden Bells" *Church Hymnal* 1951, p. 294

349 Rowe, James. "After the Midnight" *hymnary.org* https://hymnary.org/text/after_the_midnight_morning_will_greet_us

350 Rowe, James. "Won't it be Wonderful There?" *Church Hymnal* 1951, p. 358

351 Luke 16:19-31

352 Hascall, Jefferson. "O Come, Angel Band" *New Songs of Inspiration – Book Five* 1963, p. 266

353 Ramsey, Thomas. "I Won't Have to Cross Jordan Alone" *Great Gospel Songs and Hymns* 1976, p. 47

354 Gilmore, Joseph. "He Leadeth Me" *Church Hymnal* 1951, p. 335

355 Toplady, Augustus. "Rock of Ages" *Church Hymnal* 1951, p. 83

356 Rushtoi, Esther Kerr. "When We See Christ" *Worship His Majesty* 1987, p. 699

357 Lowry, Robert. "Shall We Gather at the River?" *Church Hymnal* 1951, pp. 384-385

358 Bennett, S. Fillmore. "Sweet By and By" *Church Hymnal* 1951, pp. 350-351

359 Martin, I.G. "The Eastern Gate" *Church Hymnal* 1951, p. 312

360 Brumley, Albert E. "If We Never Meet Again this Side of Heaven" *Church Hymnal* 1951, p. 36

361 Brumley, Albert E. "I'll Meet You in the Morning" *Church Hymnal* 1951, p. 14

362 Brumley, Albert E. "I'll Meet You by the River" *Church Hymnal* 1951, p. 132

363 Brumley, Albert E. "Jesus, Hold My Hand" *Church Hymnal* 1951, p. 52

364 Blair, H.E. "Meet Me There" *Songs We Sing* 1954, p. 299

365 1 Corinthians 13:12

366 Rankin, Jeremiah. "God Be With You Til We Meet Again" *Hymns for the Family of God* 1976, p. 523

367 Oatman, Johnson. "The Last Mile of the Way" *Church Hymnal* 1951, p. 382

368 Oatman, Johnson. "The Hallelujah Side" *Church Hymnal* 1951, p. 237

369 Pace, Adger M. "Glad Reunion Day" *Church Hymnal* 1951, p. 310

370 Crosby, Fanny J. "Saved by Grace" *Church Hymnal* 1951, pp. 552-353

371 Bridgewater, Mrs. A.S. "How Beautiful Heaven Must Be" *Church Hymnal* 1951, p. 105

372 Brock, Virgil P. "Beyond the Sunset" *Church Hymnal* 1951, p. 127

373 1 Corinthians 2:9

374 Wyrtzen, Don. "Finally Home" *New Springs, a division of Brentwood-Benson Music Publishing*, 1971

375 Moore, James C. "Where We'll Never Grow Old" *Church Hymnal* 1951, p. 293

376 Romans 8:18

377 Kurzenknabe, J.H. "What a Gathering That Will Be" *Church Hymnal* 1951, p. 299

378 Hewitt, E.E. "When We All Get to Heaven" *Church Hymnal* 1951, p. 393

379 Cornell, W.D. "Wonderful Peace" *Church Hymnal* 1951, p. 290

CHAPTER FIFTEEN ENDNOTES

380 Matt. 24:36-46; John14:1-3; Acts 1:9-11; 1 Cor. 15:51-58; 1 Thess. 4:13-18; Titus 2:11-14; 2 Tim. 4:6-8; Heb. 9:28; 1 John 3:1-3; Rev. 19:11-16

381 Mote, Edward. "The Solid Rock" *Worship His Majesty* 1987, p. 443

382 Frazier, Allan. "When Jesus Comes in the Clouds" *Church Hymnal* 1951, p. 296

383 Crosby, Fanny J. "Will Jesus Find Us Watching?" *Church Hymnal* 1951, p. 364

384 Black, James M. "When the Roll is Called Up Yonder" *Church Hymnal* 1951, p. 240

385 Warner, D.S. "I Know My Name is There" *Church Hymnal* 1951, p. 346

386 Luke 10:20

387 Crosby, Fanny J. "In the Twinkling of an Eye" *The Gospel Hymnal* 1973, p. 67

388 1 Thessalonians 5:23

389 Ibid.

390 1 Corinthians 15:51

391 Winsett, R.E. "In the Great Triumphant Morning" *Church Hymnal* 1951, p. 261

392 Winsett, R.E. "Jesus is Coming Soon" *Sing Unto the Lord* 1978, p. 288

393 Winsett, R.E. "Will You Meet Me Over Yonder" *Church Hymnal* 1951, p. 196

394 Roberts, Mae Taylor. "The Meeting in the Air" *Church Hymnal* 1951, p. 10

395 Thomas, J.E. "Hallelujah, We Shall Rise" *Church Hymnal* 1951, p. 272

396 Buffam, Herbert. "Lift Me Up Above the Shadows" *Church Hymnal* 1951, p.100

397 Newton, John. "Amazing Grace" *Church Hymnal* 1951, p. 57

398 Lewis, G.J. "I Can Almost Hear the Trumpets" *The Gospel Hymnal* 1973, p. 369

399 Revelation 19:11-16; 20:6

400 Kirk, J.M. "Our Lord's Return to Earth" *Church Hymnal* 1951, p. 327

401 Romans 8:19-23

402 Revelation 20:1-10

403 Wesley, Charles. "Lo, He Comes with Clouds Descending" *Church Hymnal* 1951, p. 278

404 Hine, Stuart K. "How Great Thou Art" *Worship His Majesty* 1987, p. 111

405 Spafford, Horatio. "It is Well with My Soul" *Worship His Majesty* 1987, p. 524

406 Luke 19:13

407 Hamblen, Stuart. "Until Then" *Worship His Majesty* 1987, p. 696

408 Crosby, Fanny J. "Praise Him! Praise Him!" *Worship His Majesty* 1987, p. 43

409 Crosby, Fanny J. "He Hideth My Soul" *Worship His Majesty* 1987, p. 428

410 Blackmore, C. "Some Golden Daybreak" *Hymns of Glorious Praise* 1969, p. 140

411 Jensen, Gordon. "Tears Are a Language God Understands." *New Spring Publishing* 1971

412 2 Peter 3:1-9

413 Jensen, Gordon. "Redemption Draweth Nigh" *Gospel Hymnal Volume II* 1979, p. 114

414 Whittle, Daniel. "I Know Whom I Have Believed" *Hymns for the Family of God* 1976, p. 631

415 Goodman, Rusty. "I Believe He's Coming Back (Like He Said) *Canaanland Music* 1978

416 Goodman, Charles, and Jimmie Davis. "I Wouldn't Take Nothing for My Journey" *Jimmie Davis Music Company* 1964

417 Ibid.

CHAPTER SIXTEEN ENDNOTES

418 Derricks, Cleavant. "We'll Soon Be Done with Troubles and Trials" *Church Hymnal* 1951, p. 30

419 Crosby, Fanny J. "City of Gold" *hymnary.org* https://hymnary.org/text/theres_a_city_that_looks_oer_the_valley

420 Brumley, Albert. "I'm Bound for that City" *Songs We Love* 1969, p. 90

421 Crutchfield, James Allen. "Zion's Hill" *Stamps-Baxter Gospel Hymnal* 1975, p. 120

422 Matthew 24:36

423 Watts, Isaac, "We're Marching to Zion" *Worship His Majesty* 1987, p. 550

424 Hunter, William. "I Feel Like Traveling On" *Church Hymnal* 1951, p. 133

425 Featherston, William R. "My Jesus, I Love Thee" *Hymns for the Family of God* 1976, p. 456

426 Ibid.

427 Weatherly, Frederick. "The Holy City" *james-joyce-music.com* http://www.james-joyce-music.com/song11_lyrics.html

428 Washington, Nettie Dudley. "I Bowed on My Knees and Cried Holy" *hymnary.org* https://hymnary.org/text/i_dreamed_of_that_city_called_glory

429 Rambo, Dottie. "Marvelous Grace" *New Songs of Inspiration – Number Nine* 1973, p.154

430 Rambo, Dottie. "He Looked Beyond My Fault and Saw My Need." *Rambo Music Co.* 1967

431 Rambo, Dottie. "I've Never Been this Homesick Before" *Keep on Singing* 1979, pp. 26-27

432 Rambo, Dottie. "The Holy Hills of Heaven Call Me" *Rambo Music Company* 1968

433 Rambo, Dottie. "Tears Will Never Stain the Streets" *The American Country Hymn Book* 1979, pp. 178-179

434 Rambo, Dottie. "We Shall Behold Him" *New Spring* 1980

435 Rambo, Dottie and Jimmie Davis. "Sheltered in the Arms of God" *Jimmie Davis Music Company* 1969

436 Harmon, Nancy. "I've Come too Far" *Keep On Singing* 1979, pp. 34-35

437 Tillman, Charlie. "When I Get to the End of the Way" *The Broadman Hymnal* 1940, p. 26

438 Revelation 21:1 – 22:21

439 1 Corinthians 16:22

440 Cornelius, R.H. "O, I Want to See Him" *Church Hymnal* 1951, p. 279

441 Breck, Carrie. "Face to Face" *Hymns for the Family of God* 1976, p. 128

442 Crosby, Fanny J. "My Savior First of All" *Church Hymnal* 1951, p. 320

443 Blom, Fred. "He the Pearly Gates Will Open" *Hymns for the Family of God* 1976, p. 72

444 Moore, J.L. "Sweeping Through the Gates" *Church Hymnal* 1951, p. 280

445 2 Corinthians 5:21

446 Baxter, Lydia O. "The Gate was Left Ajar for Me" *library.time-lesstruths.org* https://library.timelesstruths.org/music/The_Gate_Ajar_for_Me/

447 Hill, Jim. "What a Day That Will Be" *Worship His Majesty* 1987, p. 281

448 Speer, G.T. "Heaven's Jubilee" *Church Hymnal* 1951, p. 110

449 Gaither, William J. and Gloria. "The King is Coming" *Worship His Majesty* 1987, p. 280

450 Perronet, Edward. "All Hail the Power of Jesus' Name" *Worship His Majesty* 1987, p. 4

451 1 Kings 10:7

452 Hunter, William. "I Feel Like Traveling On" *Church Hymnal* 1951, p. 133

SPECIAL PERMISSION

At least 318 songs are referenced in *"The Dream Train."* 242 of these lyrics are in the Public Domain. In addition to these hymns, 66 songs are mentioned only by title, with no printed lyrics. The following 10 songs are also included with permission and / or license cited below:

He Lives (composed by Alfred Ackley)

"HE LIVES" Words and Music by Alfred Ackley © 1933 Curb Word Music (ASCAP) All rights administered by WC Music Corp. WC Music Corp. 100% On behalf of Curb Word Music

Some Golden Daybreak (composed by Carl Blackmore)

"SOME GOLDEN DAYBREAK" Words and Music by CARL BLACKMORE © 1934 Curb Word Music (ASCAP) All rights administered by WC Music Corp. WC Music Corp. 100% On behalf of Curb Word Musi

Then Jesus Came (composed by Oswald J. Smith)

"THEN JESUS CAME" Words and Music by Oswald J. Smith and HOMER RODEHEAVER © 1940 Curb Word Music (ASCAP) All rights administered by WC Music Corp. WC Music Corp. 100% On behalf of Curb Word Music

He Set Me Free (composed by Albert E. Brumley)

Copyright © 1939 Bridge Building Music (BMI) (adm. at CapitolCMGPublishing.com) All rights reserved. Used by permission.

Let Me Touch Him (composed by Vep Ellis)

I received permission to print these lyrics from Vep Ellis Jr. on behalf of the E.M. Ellis Family Trust.

I Know He Heard My Prayer (composed by Vep Ellis)

I received permission to print these lyrics from Vep Ellis Jr. on behalf of the E.M. Ellis Family Trust.

I'll Go (composed by Nancy Harmon)

I received written permission to print these lyrics from Nancy Harmon Ministries.

I've Come Too Far to Look Back (composed by Nancy Harmon)

I received written permission to print these lyrics from Nancy Harmon Ministries.

Redemption Draweth Nigh (composed by Gordon Jensen)

I received written permission to print these lyrics from Gordon Jensen.

An Unfinished Task (composed by Ruth Munsey)

I received written permission to print these lyrics from Ruth Munsey.